CW00802056

Knowledge Management Handbook

Other titles available from Law Society Publishing:

Client Service for Law Firms
Heather Stewart

Cloud Computing for Law Firms (due 2012)
Tim Hill

Data Protection Handbook (2nd edn)
General Editor: Peter Carey

Email: Law, Practice and Compliance
Stewart Room

Freedom of Information Handbook (3rd edn, due 2012)
General Editors: Peter Carey and Robin Hopkins

Information Sharing Handbook
Edited by Claire Bessant; Consultant Editor: Phil Tompkins

Managing People in a Legal Business
General Editor: Gill Andrew

Marketing Legal Services (2nd edn)
David Monk and Alastair Moyes

Privacy Law Handbook
Edited by Keith Mathieson

Titles from Law Society Publishing can be ordered from all good bookshops or direct (telephone 0870 850 1422, email **lawsociety@prolog.uk.com** or visit our online shop at **www.lawsociety.org.uk/bookshop**).

Knowledge Management Handbook

Hélène Russell

The Law Society

ISBN-13: 978-1-907698-11-8 (Hardback)
ISBN-13: 978-1-907698-51-4 (EPUB)

Published in 2012 by the Law Society
113 Chancery Lane, London WC2A 1PL

Typeset by Columns Design XML Ltd, Reading
Printed by TJ International Ltd, Padstow, Cornwall

The paper used for the text pages of this book is FSC certified. FSC (the Forest Stewardship Council) is an international network to promote responsible management of the world's forests.

To John, Tom and Verity

Contents

Acknowledgements

Many thanks to all those that I have met in the field of knowledge management: colleagues and friends, and those I have met briefly at conferences. I truly appreciate how they have all added to my knowledge, skill and experience in a valuable way. Thanks as well to the members of Knowledge Network West, who have provided encouragement, as well as valuable insights. They have all been fantastic. Thanks to Heather Robinson, who supported me in my first PSL role at Bevan Brittan and later as a friend. Lastly, many thanks to Simon Blackett, commissioning editor at the Law Society, who had the same vision for the book as I did, and Sarah and Gillian who led me through the editing process.

Thanks also, to my husband John, who has been unbelievably supportive and understanding, and to my kids, Tom and Verity, who might not really understand what has been going on over this last year, but who have put up with extra nursery, holiday club and camping to let me work.

Hélène Russell
June 2012

Chapter 1

Introduction: setting the scene

After reading this chapter you will appreciate:

- A few key definitions and concepts

- Some background history and key influencers

- How law firms work as people, profit and knowledge businesses

- A little about law firm challenges and how knowledge management (KM) can help

- The benefits of KM to the professional services sector

Knowledge management: an introduction

> ... the only sustainable advantage a firm has, comes from what it collectively knows, how efficiently it uses what it knows, and how readily it acquires and uses new knowledge.
>
> Davenport & Prusak *Working Knowledge*[1]

Why read this book?

Lawyers have been managing their practices and the knowledge those practices are based on for hundreds of years, without knowledge management' handbooks or specialist training, so why spend non-chargeable time reading this handbook? Is knowledge management (KM) just another business theory, great for consultants and conference organisers, but a time and money waster for practitioners?

Law firms sell their clients solutions to their problems based on their combined knowledge and experience, through their advice, representation and advocacy, and written documents. Whether they know it or not, lawyers are in the 'knowledge' business and most have been doing KM within their firms for many years. Any means by which lawyers manage their knowledge in order to be more efficient is 'knowledge management'. Law firms have always been about 'minds' not 'hands' and many will even have a KM strategy, although it probably isn't labelled as such.

Why read this book now? There is no denying that the information age has brought about a new global competitiveness, which is forcing rapid change in all business sectors. To some extent legal professionals, who practise under different laws in different nations, have been sheltered so far from many of the forces which have changed the landscape for clothing manufacturers or helpdesks, but it is doubtful whether this will last much longer.

Trends towards quality and leaner organisations have also contributed to increased interest in knowledge. As clients became more sophisticated in their understanding and use of these business methodologies, they expect their law firms to embrace similar efficiency gains. And as each generation suffers an economic downturn and loses key staff to redundancy and outsourcing, remaining staff realise how much valuable knowledge is lost and try to think of new ways to avoid this in the future.

The other side of the coin is, of course, that knowledge workers such as lawyers need new challenges to remain fulfilled in their work. While you may begin to read this book anxious that KM offers a life of standardised, commoditised work, without the intellectual challenges of bespoke legal work, I hope you will finish the book with a clear view of KM as an enabler, helping to strip out the standard, dull tasks from legal work and enabling lawyers to concentrate on the truly complex aspects of their work, the aspects that clients are prepared to pay for.

The aim of this book is to enable lawyers and those who work in support functions in the legal sector to understand the world of 'knowledge management' better so that they can improve their firm's efficiency, effectiveness and profitability, securing them for the future.

When writing this book, I had in mind some potential readers: a new Head of Knowledge at a mid-sized regional firm, probably a partner and an expert in their own specialism, but new to KM, trying to understand their firm through 'KM glasses' for the first time; a new professional support lawyer (PSL) working alone in a department, struggling to understand how best to support his team with a limited budget; and an enthusiastic new partner in a smaller firm who sees the changes to the legal landscape as a challenge and hopes to develop a new kind of law firm. This book isn't an academic book about KM and no doubt many within the profession will see gaps in the content, but my aim has been to highlight the key issues for those new to knowledge management in short chapters, then expand these with case studies, project plans and interviews. I imagine readers dipping in and out of this book perhaps on their commute or quickly reading up on topics as they need to know about them, so I have tried to keep the jargon to a minimum and the concepts easy to digest.

The rise of knowledge management in other business sectors

Key people and influencers

Knowledge management as a business theory began to come to prominence in the 1980s, although it wasn't until the 1990s that it became popular.

As with many business theories, a number of business leaders began asking similar questions at around the same time. In the early 1980s, Karl-Erik Sveiby began questioning why the balance sheet for his business had plenty of typewriters and desks, but little (one krona) for the value of his brand and nothing for its intangible assets. These ideas were published in a book *The Invisible Balance Sheet*[2] in 1986 and soon other companies in Scandinavia took notice and began to amend their procedures.

In the legal profession, Magic Circle firms began to experiment with knowledge specialists in the early 1980s. Initially this was simply a move to formalise precedent databases and consolidate work and styles across offices, but later, influenced by the success stories in manufacturing, software, pharmaceuticals and accountancy, it began to investigate and adopt other aspects of KM.

BOX 1.1   Key influencers

Verna Allee – author of *The Knowledge Evolution: Expanding Organizational Intelligence*.

Peter Drucker – management consultant and prolific writer; coined the term 'knowledge worker' in 1959.

David Gurteen – creator of the 'Knowledge café'.

Ikujiro Nonaka – Matsushita software designer, co-author of *The Knowledge-Creating Company* and creator of the knowledge spiral.

Peter Senge – author of *The Fifth Discipline*.

David Snowden – ex-IBM and founder of Cognitive Edge Pty Ltd.

Karl-Erik Sveiby – co-author of *The Invisible Balance Sheet*.

What is knowledge management?

Many people dislike the term 'knowledge management'. How can you 'manage' a company's collective 'knowledge'? Knowledge isn't a widget on a production line. However, until a better description emerges, we are stuck with it.

There are many different definitions of KM. These will be covered in depth in Chapter 2, but to set the scene, my own working definition, an amalgamation of a number of different definitions, is:

the business process by which knowledge of many kinds is created, harvested, analysed, stored, leveraged, retrieved and retired, in order to further a business's goals.

The important things to note are that:

- There are different kinds of 'knowledge'.
- There are different ways to 'manage' it, including creating and destroying it.
- Information technology (IT) can be part of the solution but KM ≠ IT.
- The purpose of managing knowledge is to support a business's goals.

The business of law firms

Law firms are different to other businesses and it is useful to consider the business of law firms in order to later consider how KM can help to make these businesses more efficient, effective and profitable.[3]

Law firms can be divided into profit businesses, people businesses and knowledge businesses.[4]

Profit businesses

Law firms are in business to make a profit. They have a particular structure, the partnership structure, and they measure their profits by profit per equity partner (PPEP). Traditionally PPEP was simply calculated by dividing total profit (revenue less expenses) by the number of equity partners. However this told partners nothing about the drivers of PPEP, so in 1993, David Maister[5] described four drivers of PPEP:

PPEP=average realised rate x leverage x margin x utilisation

where:

- Average realised rate is the average hourly rate achieved by the firm, calculated by dividing total billings by the number of hours billed.
- Leverage describes the proportion of partners to non-partners. This is assumed to be a measure of experienced to non-experienced staff, but is not really, as some coal-face lawyers are far more technically adept than many equity partners who have other non-technical skills, but measuring experience levels would be difficult. Leverage is the total number of lawyers in a team or department divided by the number of equity partners (i.e. ten lawyers in a department, divided into two teams each headed by an equity partner, gives a leverage in each team of five (5/1) and department of five (10/2).

- Margin measures profitability as a percentage and is calculated by dividing the profit of a team by the fees charged. The profit is its revenues less the direct and indirect expenses related to it.
- Utilisation is the average billable hours recorded by the fee earners in a team or department (i.e. total billable hours for the team divided by the number of fee earners).

Maister describes the first two measures (average realised rate and leverage) as health issues and the second two (margin and utilisation) as hygiene issues.

Improving hygiene factors is relatively straightforward: cutting costs (improve margin) or working people harder (utilisation). However, you can only get so far in improving profit by encouraging your fee earners to work harder or sacrificing expenses and there is always the risk that it will damage quality of services, driving away clients, and be unpopular with employees, leading to loss of talent.

To improve profitability further, you will need to work smarter not harder and improve health factors. This is more difficult to achieve, but provides a sustainable improvement in profitability in the longer term and it is here that KM techniques can particularly help improve a firm's profitability.

People businesses

Law firms have always been about minds, not widgets. People are a law firm's main asset and they are its greatest expense and so a firm needs to ensure it is maximising the return on its investment. KM can help by attracting talented lawyers, ensuring they stay interested in their work and remain with the firm.[6]

Knowledge businesses

Law firms sell knowledge. For years that has been enough, but now, with the rise of the information age, much of the legal information that lawyers base their work on is readily available and easily accessible from one's home. However, note the phrase 'information age'. This is an age of excessive amounts of easily accessible information. What lawyers do for clients is to understand that information and apply their training and experience to it, to provide workable solutions to clients' problems. What they sell is not access to information, but wisdom, tacit knowledge, judgement, creativity, understanding and sense-making.

The benefits of knowledge management to law firms

KM enables best practice to be commoditised to leverage information from the most expensive experienced fee earners, down to the lowest appropriate member of staff. It facilitates faster retrieval of known facts, consistency, quality and best practice. It also shortens the lead-in time for new starters and enables them to tap into the firm's best practice and firm style at an early point. Also, if new work is done on 'hot topics' or new knowledge created, KM allows a wide variety of fee earners to tap into that and sell it to more clients.

The issue of staff retention isn't such an issue now, but five years ago there was a real battle for talented junior staff. A developed KM system helps with attracting and maintaining staff, as it strips out the dull parts of the job, enabling them to concentrate on more rewarding work, and minimises non-chargeable administration and write-offs, which improves their figures. Also talented lawyers will always be in demand whatever the economic situation and bored lawyers look elsewhere.

What is probably more of an issue these days is retaining knowledge and experience within a firm when people leave. It used to be that KM professionals discussed how best to harvest an individual's knowledge when they happily moved on or retired, but as more and more partners are being encouraged to retire early, are edged out and staff made redundant, it is becoming far more important to retain knowledge throughout the working life of individuals, not rely on gathering that knowledge as they leave. Given that people are leaving under less than happy circumstances and that knowledge is power in law firms, people are taking what they can with them.

Employee cynicism is also devastating for businesses. If staff see inexperienced fee earners being promoted and legal expertise ignored, the negative culture that this creates can destroy a firm's reputation. Whilst skills other than legal expertise are obviously important to clients, what is the point of a commercially savvy lawyer whose documents are unenforceable or whose settlement offer is derided? Clients expect a certain level of expertise and staff need to see that expertise is valued and recognised.

Lastly, KM can help with client retention. Successful KM initiatives ensure all fee earners are up to date and offering high quality, current, relevant, effective advice to clients, which obviously keeps them happy and coming back for more. Secondly, firms have also been offering client-focused KM as a value-add, i.e. offering a research facility, an e-portal with current awareness or other relevant information. It will be interesting to see whether this trend continues. More firms are chasing less work so they will wish to continue to offer such facilities, but with margins squeezed, they may not be able to afford to.

Whatever the business strategy of the law firm, there are aspects that KM theory and practice can help with.

The emergence of KM within the English legal landscape

Lawyers have been doing KM since lawyering began, but it wasn't until the 1960s that know-how in law firms was particularly discussed, and not until the early 1980s that law firms began to develop formal knowledge collections.

In the mid 1980s commentators started to talk of law firms as knowledge businesses and in the 1990s know-how gained momentum in law firms with the rise of the information age, improvements in information technology and the influence of KM in other sectors.

There are different ideas as to why knowledge management emerged at that point. Some believe that the legal sector absorbed business ideas from different sectors, under pressure to become more lean, others believe that it was a response to the combination of economic pressure and increased numbers of women in the profession, as creating part-time KM roles enabled law firms to hold on to female rainmakers whilst their children were young.

BOX 1.2   Historical development of knowledge management

1980s to 1990s – consolidation of precedent collections.

1995 – 'what is knowledge?' academic focus.

1997 – focus on measurement – all kinds of methods were tried (Intellectual Capital Measurement Model, the Skandia Navigator, the Intangible Assets Monitor, the Inclusive Valuation Methodology) but no one method became standard and often they seemed to create as many problems as they solved.

1998 – focus on communities of practice and building a knowledge-sharing culture.

2000 – after action learning.

2002–03 – business strategy focus.

2005 – client-facing KM developed – a means of firms differentiating themselves and offering a value-add to clients.

2006 – social media (blogs and wikis, even Second Life).

Today – outsourcing is a growing trend and there has been a return to measurement and business strategy focus.

Initially most KM work took the form of creating formalised databases of precedents, codifying existing knowledge. Later, once this task was as complete as possible,[7] knowledge workers turned their attention to law firm culture, to the need to change practice to encourage the sharing of knowledge amongst fee earners. There has always been an in-built opposition to knowledge sharing within law firms, because the sharing of knowledge benefits the firm, but disadvantages the fee earner (KM work is usually non-chargeable) a problem that continues to affect most firms today.

KM and the legal sector today

As we emerge from one recession and face the possibility of another or years of stagflation, there are many different challenges to law firms, not least the government's wish to widen access to legal services by creating alternative business systems (ABS), also known as 'Tesco law'. The risk often raised in relation to ABS is that supermarkets will use their lean methods to hive off easily commoditised work, such as conveyancing and wills, the bread and butter work of High Street law firms, and potential clients will favour big brands they already know and trust over small High Street firms.

Law firms also face other significant challenges (cuts to legal aid, changes to funding of civil claims, information overload, old habits v new challenges, resources shortfalls, staff resistance, technology failure, etc.). KM can help the professional services sector improve profitability, efficiency and effectiveness, and to attract and retain talented staff, retain knowledge, retain clients, improve cross-selling, innovation and risk management.

Summary: the least you should know

- Knowledge has always been the key asset for law firms and lawyers have been 'doing knowledge management' for decades.
- Knowledge management grew as a separate business theory in the 1990s and is now embedded within large firms.
- Knowledge management is the business process by which knowledge of many kinds is created, harvested, analysed, stored, leveraged, retrieved and retired, in order to further a business's strategic goals.
- Knowledge management can help all firms become more efficient, effective and profitable.

ANNEX 1A: The seven deadly sins of knowledge management

You will probably find it useful to revisit these seven deadly sins of KM after you have finished this book and during some of your KM projects.

1. Failure to link KM strategy to business strategy or failure to have any KM strategy at all.
2. Assuming that KM = IT.
3. Ignoring the culture problem.
4. Choosing a top-down or bottom-up approach.
5. Setting unrealistic deadlines and budgets.
6. Trying to codify too much and/or ignoring the sharing of tacit knowledge.
7. Failure to communicate 'the point' of KM to the firm at large and failure to measure and communicate successes.

Endnotes

1 Davenport, T. and Prusak, L. (2000) *Working Knowledge* Harvard Business Press, Introduction, p. xxiv.
2 Sveiby, K. (1990) *Den Osynliga Balansrakningen*, Affarsvarlden Forlag. Now out of print. Further details at **www.sveiby.com/library.html**.
3 This topic is covered in more depth in Chapter 9.
4 Thanks to Juliet Humphries, then of Perian Spring, for bringing this idea to my attention.
5 Maister, D. (2003) *Managing the Professional Services Firm*, Simon & Schuster UK Ltd, Chapter 3.
6 Law Ladders recruitment found in their survey of November 2011 that 52% of senior lawyers surveyed would leave their jobs if they got bored, despite the downturn. Although an informal survey by a recruitment agency, it illustrates a problem that will resonate with all senior practice managers.
7 See Chapters 2, 5 and 6 for a discussion about what can and can't be codified.

Chapter 2

What is knowledge?

After reading this chapter, you will understand:

■ Some of the academic background and theory behind knowledge management

■ How to divide 'knowledge' in a number of different ways in order to:

   – understand better what you are trying to 'manage'
   – understand the most appropriate ways to 'manage' it

■ What the 'knowledge cycle' is

■ How 'knowledge management' has been defined

■ Some of the problems with the definitions, so that you can avoid common pitfalls when applying these in practice

---

Knowledge: what is it?

The aim of this chapter is to help you to understand the language used by knowledge management (KM) professionals and the ways that KM professionals divide 'knowledge' into different types. This is a useful process because it will enable you to:

• provide the most appropriate solution for each particular kind of 'knowledge';
• be strategic and focus on managing the type of 'knowledge' that gives you greatest return on investment;
• cope with information overload.

Most lawyers instinctively understand what is meant by knowledge, but there are a couple of ways of defining knowledge used by KM professionals that are particularly useful for lawyers to understand.

This chapter will look at:

1. the DIK(W) pyramid;
2. explicit v tacit; and

3. knowledge in terms of function.

When reading this chapter, the most important thing to bear in mind is that the purpose of KM in law firms is to create better, more profitable law firms. KM isn't an end in itself. I have introduced these terms here because they will probably be helpful, but if they aren't, ignore them and use terms that suit you and your firm.

DIK(W) pyramid

For many years information science literature has divided 'knowledge' in the broad sense into data, information and knowledge. Some commentators add wisdom as a top layer, or even insight, resolve, etc., but more recently, most include wisdom within knowledge.[1] This has been adopted into the European Framework for Knowledge Management.[2]

Figure 2.1   Data, information knowledge and wisdom (the DIK(W) pyramid)

Data

This is[3] a set of discrete objective facts: numbers, symbols, figures. They are self-contained and, in isolation, have little if any meaning.

For example, one morning, a woman goes to an independent newsagent and buys a newspaper and a pint of milk. The data of that transaction may be:

*   which newspaper she buys and whether it is a daily or weekly paper, a broadsheet or tabloid;
*   which brand and type of milk she buys;

- whether the milk was on a special offer or not;
- what payment method she used;
- what both items cost.

None of this data tells anyone working for the newsagent why that customer chose that shop, whether or when she will be back, whether she acts as an ambassador and recommends the shop to friends, whether the shop is profitable in the short or long term and why that is.

Information

Once the data is arranged and assembled and context is added, information is created.[4] Information is data that makes a difference: data that informs the receiver of something. It is a message.

In the newsagent example, if someone looks at all the transactions in the morning, or looks at all of that woman's transactions as a historical group and analyses how and when she uses the shop, they will have gathered information about her data. The information sends a message to them about her custom.

Knowledge

Knowledge is broader and deeper than information. Knowledge is a valuable asset which can be used to aid decision-making. It is difficult to define, but generally when meaning is added by the receiver to the information which makes it actionable, knowledge is created. As the meaning is added by an individual based on their experiences to date, knowledge is highly personal. Information is a flow of messages, and knowledge is created by that flow within the beliefs of the receiver. Knowledge can be explicit or tacit,[5] individual or collective. Knowledge is both a flow and a stock, an act and an artefact.

Davenport and Prusak give their working definition of 'knowledge' as:

> a fluid mix of framed experience, values, contextual information, and expert insight that provides a framework for evaluating and incorporating new experiences and information. It originates and is applied in the minds of knowers. In organisations, it often becomes embedded not only in documents and repositories but also in organizational routines, processes, practices, and norms.[6]

Davenport and Prusak describe four ways (the four Cs) for 'information' to become 'knowledge',[7] all of which require human input:

- Comparison: how does information about this situation compare to other situations we have known?
- Consequences: what implications does the information have for decision-making?

- Connections: how does this bit of knowledge relate to others?
- Conversation: what do other people think about this information?

Knowledge is only created in the mind of the receiver. It is therefore possible for someone to believe they are imparting 'knowledge' but the receiver believes it is only 'information' because of their respective contexts. As a result of this, knowledge tends to be 'sticky'[8] and tends only to thrive in the environment that developed it.

In the newsagent example, if a staff member looked at all the information about when women shop for staples generally and when women use that newsagent specifically, they may be able to reach a conclusion about when and why women use their shop, such as 'Few women use our newsagent at night. Women do use the supermarket further down the road at night for staples. Our shop front is poorly lit and we are reliant on on-street parking. The supermarket is brighter, more welcoming and has reliable parking. If we spend some money on improving our lighting we may improve our sales in this underperforming segment.'

In the legal sector, in relation to technical legal knowledge, one can see how lawyers with experience can analyse the facts of a situation against their knowledge of legal statutes and case law using all these four means, to give advice to a client about appropriate next steps in their situation.

Wisdom

Wisdom is not always included in the pyramid, but some say it is broader and deeper still than knowledge. It is the result of adding insight and experience to knowledge. Many KM academics find this distinction unhelpful and do not put wisdom separately in the pyramid but include it in knowledge.

If one is going to consider wisdom separately, in the newsagent example, the wisdom might be that an experienced member of staff recalls that the previous owners tried something similar ten years ago, which didn't work, although no one understood why. However, she concludes that there is something about the shop's layout – which she instinctively understands based on her years of experience but which is difficult to explain (perhaps a combination of a number of different factors: lighting, distance from street lights, positioning of shelves, shadows from neighbouring buildings, etc.) – which puts women off at night, none of which can be changed without significant cost. As a result they should concentrate their marketing efforts elsewhere until the shop is wholly refurbished, when a detailed cost-benefit analysis can be undertaken.

It is probably clear to you how these definitions are helpful in manufacturing or retail industries, but are they helpful in a knowledge business, such as a law firm, where the product is rarely data or information, but knowledge (and wisdom)?

This DIK(W) pyramid can be useful in law firms to help to decide what kind of solution is needed in a particular situation and to focus on getting the greatest return on investment.

For example, a firm has two priorities at present:

1. it is beginning a policy of transparent career paths and as a starting point, wants to ensure that all staff have access to the firm's human resources (HR) procedures, job descriptions and promotions criteria; and

2. it wants to find a way to cascade the experience of a partner, who would like to retire in a year or two, to more junior members of staff.

If that firm begins by considering what kind of knowledge is involved in each situation, the solution becomes clearer. A firm's HR procedures are likely to be information. How these procedures can be interpreted by the firm may be knowledge rather than information, but the codes themselves are probably information. Information can be easily codified and made available on an intranet or through an online database. The partner's years of experience on the other hand, will be knowledge (and possibly wisdom) which isn't always easy to codify to put in a database and, once codified, is not easy to access, so a different solution will be needed. A person-to-person solution (mentoring, supervision, post-transaction review meetings in small groups, etc.) would be ideal, but if the knowledge needs to be captured on a database somehow, a different method should be used to collect the knowledge (such as person-to-person interviews), and a different means of communicating with the end user would be needed (such as a collection of anecdotes annexed to practice notes or precedents).

These definitions may also be useful in law firms for studying client management (Who is a key client? Who pays bills quickly? Who is instructing us regularly? Who is instructing us with the most profitable work?) and staff performance management (Who logs the most time? Who logs the most chargeable time? Who bills the most? Whose bills are paid in full?), where both data and information are required in order to make judgements about practice management.

Historically, some law firms tried to label everything within the firm as data, information, knowledge or wisdom and found it hugely time-consuming with no real benefit to the business. The point of these definitions is to act as analytical tools to help firms with business-related goals. Don't make the definitions a goal in themselves. If they aren't helping your firm with its business goals, don't use them.

The controversy

The DIK(W) pyramid has been used extensively in computer and information science for years and has been particularly useful as a managerial model to explain how one makes use of business data inputs. Its use within KM has, however, been controversial. The difficulty has been the linearity and hierarchy of the model, particularly the idea that knowledge is created from information and that 'wisdom' exists at all.[9]

It is said that knowledge systems within businesses are far more complex than this pyramid suggests. The danger of this model is that it encourages people to think of knowledge as a thing, not a flow, and encourages businesses to concentrate their efforts on managing data and information and trying to control knowledge through ICT (which can be costly and wasteful) rather than facilitating interactions, where knowledge can flow from person to person (a more effective way of exploiting knowledge).

Explicit versus tacit and the SECI model

A definition which is less controversial and is particularly useful to lawyers is 'explicit v tacit knowledge'. This was introduced by Nonaka et al in 1991[10] and again in 1995.[11]

Explicit knowledge is codifiable knowledge. It is objective facts and figures. It can be expressed in words and numbers and can be easily written down, communicated and shared. It takes the form of hard data, scientific formulae, codified procedures or universal principles. It is the things that are known, that can easily be explained in words.

Tacit knowledge is expertise. It is highly personal and hard to formalise. It is subjective insights, intuitions and hunches based on experiences. It is hard to express, process, capture or codify. It is knowing how to react to a situation where many variables are involved. It is often difficult to express in words. It is particularly difficult to codify tacit knowledge because it is so contextual and has so much embedded knowledge. Think for yourself how difficult it is to learn to swim or ride a bike by reading a book. The easiest way to learn to do both is by one-to-one experiential learning, swimming or riding together with a teacher who offers nuggets of advice in small batches, nudging you towards a good technique.

Tacit knowledge includes intuition. Karl Weick calls intuition 'compressed expertise'[12] which is an excellent description of what most clients buy from lawyers: their ability to sum up a situation quickly and recommend a course of action that is likely to succeed within the parameters they have been given, based on their training, knowledge and experience. A lawyer may not necessarily follow a defined process in reaching a recommendation and they may not always be able to explain the subtle experiences that add up to his/her decision, but that doesn't mean that the advice is not valuable, just that the expertise is so compressed that sometimes it is difficult to articulate.

The boundary between tacit and explicit isn't always as clear as these definitions suggest, but these two definitions ring true with the lawyers that I talk to. Again, though, the purpose of dividing knowledge in this way is to help to focus on the best management strategy for the knowledge in order to further a firm's business goals, not to create work for Knowledge Lawyers. If the definitions don't work for your firm, ensure you understand them, but leave them aside.

The DIK(W) pyramid doesn't always fit nicely into 'explicit' and 'tacit' categories, but in general, they probably fit like this:

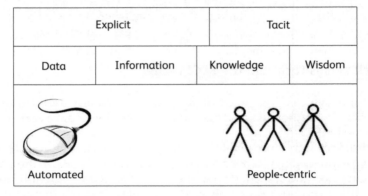

Explicit		Tacit	
Data	Information	Knowledge	Wisdom
Automated		People-centric	

Figure 2.2 Explicit and tacit knowledge within the DIK(W) pyramid

The tacit and explicit division, as with the DIK(W) pyramid, again, is useful when considering solutions to KM problems. Explicit knowledge can generally be written down and shared. It can be retained in a database, on an intranet or in paper files in a library and easily accessed and understood by others. Tacit knowledge on the other hand is difficult, although not impossible, to capture in a database, but can be more easily passed on in a small-scale training session or supervision session, peer assist programme, a Q&A or knowledge cafe.

Knowing about these definitions helps you to choose the most cost-effective solution to your knowledge problem.

The SECI model: knowledge spiral

How tacit and explicit knowledge interact

The knowledge-spiral will be considered again in Chapter 7, Training and Learning, but is discussed here to explain how tacit and explicit knowledge are transferred between people and how explicit knowledge is transformed into tacit knowledge and vice versa. Again, it is important to understand this in order to decide how best to manage these different kinds of knowledge and how best to develop systems within your law firm to exploit your fee earners' knowledge creation potential to improve profitability.

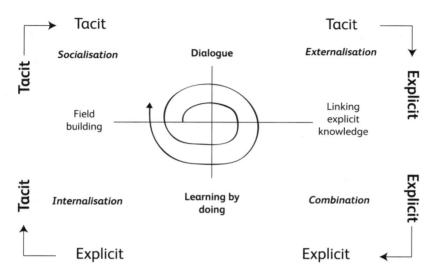

Figure 2.3   The Knowledge Spiral

(Reproduced by permission of Oxford University Press, Inc., from Ikujiro Nonaka and Hirotaka Takeuchi (1995) The Knowledge-Creating Company, p.71)

The background to this knowledge spiral begins in Japan in 1985, when the Matsushita Electrical Company could not get its bread maker to work properly. The crust came out burnt, but the inside was raw. A software developer named Ikuko Tanaka suggested working side-by-side with a famous baker at the Osaka International Hotel. Working alongside the baker, she learned his special way of stretching the dough, which inspired her to work with the Matsuishita engineers to develop special ribs inside the bread machine to stretch the dough. The knowledge spiral is a pictorial description of how the Matsuishita Electrical Company created a new kind of bread maker (new 'knowledge').

The spiral is divided into four quadrants: socialisation, externalisation, combination and internalisation, showing how knowledge is created within businesses.

The top left quadrant of the spiral is socialisation, which shows how Tanaka learned about bread-making from the baker. Socialisation is about on-the-job training, one at a time, transferring existing tacit knowledge from one person (the baker and current expert) to the new staff member (Tanaka).

The top right quadrant of the spiral, externalisation, shows how Tanaka articulated her new knowledge to the engineers. Externalisation is about making tacit knowledge explicit, usually through dialogue, using metaphors and analogies. This is people-to-people feedback and exchange of ideas.

The bottom right quadrant of the spiral, combination, shows how the engineers shared and developed knowledge amongst themselves, through documents, databases, editing knowledge and combining it with existing documents, making it transferable across groups in the organisation.[13]

Lastly, the bottom left quadrant of the spiral, internalisation, shows how the engineers and Tanaka internalised the explicit knowledge into their own personal tacit knowledge, interpreting it in the light of their own knowledge and experiences and adding it to their existing knowledge, for re-use in the next project.

The important thing to note about the knowledge spiral, especially when considering tacit and explicit knowledge and how best to support these in a business setting, is that, of the four quadrants, only one is particularly suited to transfer through IT (combination), the others are people-centric. If a firm focuses its KM activity on a knowledge-sharing database, the tacit to explicit quadrant, it misses out three-quarters of its opportunities for knowledge creation.

Most KM practitioners use Nonaka's knowledge spiral as a useful tool rather than a complete model, given the weakness in externalisation and its basis in Japanese manufacturing business, with its particular cultural context. It is also important to remember that it was also only ever meant to explain how tacit knowledge could be made explicit for a single purpose (bread maker design) to take place. Nonaka never suggested that all the tacit knowledge within the designers' heads could or should be made explicit.

An ecological model

Dave Snowden, chief scientific officer and founder of Cognitive Edge Pty Ltd, advocates a move away from the structured directive thinking and systems dynamics which has transferred from information systems thinking into KM within business, and recommends a move towards an approach based on natural sciences. He believes that humans work best in a cycle of order and chaos and that too much structure prevents new ideas and practices from emerging. Utilising a metaphor about chefs and recipe books, he recommends that KM practitioners should focus on the intuitive understanding of the chef, rather than creating the perfect recipe book.

Snowden recommends[14] that KM practitioners who work with and support those who work with complex levels of knowledge, such as lawyers, understand and work with seven heuristics:[15]

1. *Knowledge can only be volunteered it cannot be conscripted* – whilst a business can measure process compliance or information transfer, it can never determine if an employee has truly passed on all their knowledge and experience. This means that systems which connect people are more effective than systems which contain content.

2. *We only know what we know when we need to know it* – human knowledge is deeply contextual and requires stimulus for recall. This means that bringing a number of people together from different backgrounds increases the chances of the 'aha' moment that is necessary to recall the knowledge needed. It also means that when designing best practice documents or in law firms, precedents, (he isn't completely against these in appropriate circumstances), people won't always include all necessary details because they won't be appropriately stimulated to remember all relevant points, so a firm needs a wide variety of inputs to precedents to make them more complete.

3. *In the context of real need, few people will withhold their knowledge* – people will rarely refuse to share their knowledge with a co-worker to help them with a problem, but they will resist codifying all they know for the business itself. Again, this means that investments made by a business to link people encourages the flow of knowledge far better than efforts to fill databases full of more and more knowledge.

4. *Everything is fragmented* – humans naturally respond well to fragmented knowledge. Creating and using structured documents requires considerable effort, far more than scanning numerous fragmented narratives. This suggests that businesses should invest less time in preparing the perfect best practice document or precedent and more time capturing small snippets of experiences, including pictures and field notes. Lawyers can use this to improve their KM activity by putting more effort into adding snippets to practice notes than trying to perfect a precedent before publication.

5. *Tolerated failure imprints learning better than success* – avoidance of failure has greater evolutionary advantage than imitation of success. This means that firms should concentrate on sharing anecdotes about failure rather than sharing best practice systems. This isn't easy to do and requires a very special non-confrontational supportive culture which few law firms do well, so he recommends that practitioners share stories about archetypes, rather than individuals.

6. *The way we know things is not the way we report we know things* – people report that they use a structured process-oriented approach in decision-making, but in fact use heuristics, past-pattern matching and extrapolation. For other sectors this may mean developing clothing-based rituals rather than health and safety training. For law firms this suggests that case study discussions along the lines of 'Do you remember when we were in X, we did Y?' are more effective than traditional training.

7. *We always know more than we can say and we will always say more than we*

can write down – the process of taking things from our heads and putting it into a paper or a database involves the loss of content and context. For law firms, this shows how, whilst there are matters which can be written down, facilitating conversations is a more valuable means of knowledge-sharing.

In order to improve its use of complex knowledge, Snowden recommends that a business such as a law firm focuses on three heuristics (numbers 1, 2 and 7) and connects people to each other, rather than connecting them to databases. He recommends the use of best practice and precedents in appropriate situations, but for the rest, recommends investment in:

- narrative databases (especially useful for retiring employees) where stories are captured and searches encourage serendipitous encounters;
- social network stimulation, encouraging the flow of knowledge in a self-selecting way;
- disruptive pattern breaking, whereby entrenched thinking in groups is disrupted by unexpected material (such as historical stories) which creates a new perspective.

Importantly, Snowden advises businesses to study effectiveness rather than efficiency because in complex natural systems (such as business environments like law firms where humans undertake complex work requiring expertise and experience) a degree of inefficiency actually improves effectiveness.

Other useful definitions

Knowledge has been divided in a number of other ways. The following three examples are some of the other ways that seem to be useful to law firms:

In terms of its function[16]

1. Declarative knowledge (knowledge about).
2. Procedural knowledge (know-how).
3. Causal (know why).
4. Conditional (know when).
5. Relational (know with).

As a combination of individual and collective, explicit and tacit

1. Conscious (individual/explicit).
2. Automatic (individual/implicit).
3. Objectified (social/explicit).
4. Collective (social/implicit).[17]

As 'five images'

1. Embrained (dependent on conceptual skills and cognitive abilities).
2. Embodied (action-oriented and likely to be only partly explicit).
3. Encultured (the process of achieving shared understandings).
4. Embedded (knowledge which resides in systemic routines).
5. Encoded (information conveyed by signs and symbols).[18]

Which definition is better for helping a law firm make sound decisions about KM for its business needs will depend upon the nature of that firm, its employees and culture.

For many law firms, the simple explicit-tacit definition is the most useful and commonly used, although an awareness of the others, especially Dave Snowden's seven heuristics, can be helpful.

All the definitions help businesses in different ways to avoid falling into the traps previous businesses have fallen into in relation to KM, in particular a focus on costly IT and codification and a lack of focus on connecting people and facilitating networks of discussions, which characterised KM in the 1980s and 1990s and was costly and ineffective once a baseline of codification had been reached.

The knowledge cycle

Whatever knowledge may be, it is said to go through the stages set out in Figure 2.4 during its lifetime. This is the knowledge cycle, which information professionals and knowledge management professionals are expected to manage. There is a more detailed representation of this knowledge cycle in Figure 2.5, but this simplified version is a good place to begin an understanding of what knowledge is and how it is managed.

One of the important aspects to note about the knowledge cycle is the importance of the last stage – destruction and adaption. If you ignore this last phase, your fee earners will begin to distrust the validity of the knowledge in your system and begin to suffer information overload, making them less efficient in finding the right piece of knowledge for their work.

Knowledge management

The definition of 'knowledge management', like the definition of 'knowledge', is still subject to debate and to some extent the definition proposed depends upon the perspective of the proposer (sociological, technological and economic).

What KM isn't, is probably clearer than what it is.

KM definitely isn't IT systems, although IT can support many KM aims. It isn't having professional support lawyers (PSLs). It isn't understanding

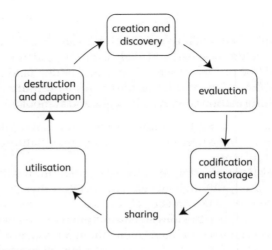

Figure 2.4   The knowledge cycle

web 2.0 and having collaborative worksites. Magic Circle firms may not have begun formally developing KM systems until the 1980s, and lawyers may not have talked about KM until the 1990s, but lawyers have been 'doing' KM in practical terms since lawyering began.

Many people dislike the term 'knowledge management'. 'Knowledge' isn't something static, so how can it be 'managed'? The idea of managing an entire business's collective knowledge from all its employees with their varied backgrounds, education and experiences seems impossible, but there is no doubt that efforts within the KM sphere have business benefits, so it has to have some form of title and so, until a better description emerges, it is practical to stick with 'knowledge management'.

The British Standards Institute has published a guide to good practice in knowledge management which uses a definition developed by Royal Dutch/Shell.[19] Knowledge management is:

> The capabilities by which communities within an organisation capture the knowledge that is critical to them, constantly improve it and make it available in the most effective manner to those people who need it, so that they can exploit it creatively to add value as part of their work.

In simple terms, KM is at the very heart of law firms and is how firms create, capture, access, apply, interpret and utilise the combined knowledge of their employees to improve their businesses. It is about the transfer and sharing of good practice; it is about sharing ideas and practice systems in order to leverage staff; it is about personal and organisational learning; it is about management of a firm's intellectual property. It is successful law firm management.

The important things to note are that:

- There are different kinds of 'knowledge'.
- There are different ways to 'manage' it, not forgetting creating and destroying it.
- Information technology (IT) can be part of the solution but KM ≠ IT.
- The aim of managing the knowledge is to support the business's goals, to give a competitive advantage.

The European Framework for Knowledge Management provides a useful holistic view,[20] placing business processes at its core, but including all players in the value chain, as knowledge is identified, created, stored, shared and used.

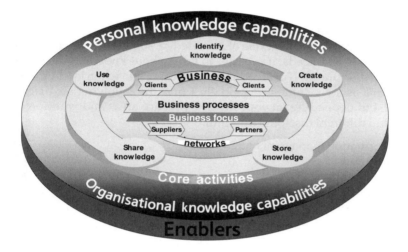

Figure 2.5 European KM Framework

(Source: CEN workshop agreement – CWA/14924-2, © March 2004.)

Lastly, one of my favourite definitions sees KM as:

the bottling of the secret sauce of knowledge, that keeps clients coming back to you.[21]

KM exists, and will continue to exist in some guise, because knowledge businesses want to improve their businesses, particularly their profitability. It is probably best to see KM as a convenient umbrella term covering all kinds of knowledge-based activities which promote increased efficiency, effectiveness, profitability and client satisfaction.

Don't get caught up in categorising all your knowledge as an end in itself or spend months on the perfect definition of KM in your firm. These different definitions have been outlined here simply to help you to:

- understand KM professionals and read further into the subject if you need to;
- think about knowledge within your firm from different angles, to help you to exploit it to improve your business;
- avoid semantic drift or mission creep, so that your KM initiatives don't become information initiatives;
- avoid too many aspects of firm management becoming the KM department's responsibility, without the matching budget.

Knowledge activities as six disciplines

Lastly, instead of dividing knowledge into different types or basing a definition around the life cycle of knowledge, sometimes when studying a whole firm's KM needs, it is easier to think about knowledge activities as different disciplines. This is certainly something I do when looking at KM in law firms as a consultant. Personally I find the following six disciplines useful, but depending on your firm, its practice areas and workforce, you may find different disciplines helpful:

- Information management and search.
- Workflow.
- Collaboration.
- Training/learning.
- Networking.
- Client-facing KM.

Again, use these definitions as they help your firm. They can be helpful headings for reviewing KM processes as part of an audit or strategy development or a checklist to make sure that other reviews have reached all important parts of the business.

Summary: the least you need to know

■ Knowledge is the most important asset a law firm has.

■ It is easier for the knowledge to be managed in a law firm if it is divided up:

  – Knowledge can be divided into explicit (objective facts) and tacit (subjective insights); or
  – Knowledge can also be divided under the DIK(W) pyramid.

■ Knowledge management is how firms create, capture, access, apply, interpret and utilise the combined knowledge of their employees to improve their businesses.

■ Knowledge activity can be divided into six disciplines (networking, learning, information management and search, workflow, client-facing KM and collaboration).

■ Don't waste time with definitions. Use the definitions to help you to decide upon solutions to knowledge problems and to further business objectives, not as an end in themselves.

ANNEX 2A: Ten KM commandments

1.   Think and act strategically.
2.   Focus on business needs and always start from business strategy.
3.   Measure results and act upon those metrics.
4.   Ensure there is strong top-down support for KM initiatives.
5.   Ensure there is strong, respected leadership within KM.
6.   Educate staff so they understand why knowledge-sharing is valuable to the business and how it is in their and everyone else's interest.
7.   Once you have the ICT basics in place and have codified an appropriate amount of knowledge, concentrate on connecting people for maximum sharing of valuable tacit knowledge.
8.   Have your own definition of knowledge and knowledge management, but don't let definitions and categorisations become an end in themselves.
9.   Support knowledge sharing by appropriate recognition and reward structures.
10.   Remember that KM ≠ IT and KM ≠ information management or law libraries. KM is about how your firm can meet its business objectives, whether that is to be more efficient, more effective and/or more profitable.

Endnotes

1   Chapter 1 of Davenport and Prusak's *Working Knowledge* (2000) gives an excellent description of this DIK(W) pyramid. I have explained the main salient points, but it is worth reading their sections for more depth.
2   Mekhilef, M., Olesen, A.J. and Kelleher, D. (2003) *European Guide to Good Practice in Knowledge Management*, Chapter 1, Terminology.
3   Data is a plural noun, but I have adopted the more common singular usage.
4   Davenport and Prusak (2000), p. 4. Davenport & Prusak describe five ways that data can be converted into information (the five 'C's): contextualisation, categorisation, calculation, correction, and condensation.
5   Ibid, p. 7.
6   Ibid, p. 5.
7   Ibid, p. 6.
8   Ibid, p. 56.
9   Dave Snowden has even threatened (humorously I hope) to shoot those who talk about 'wisdom' as a higher level of knowledge ('DIKW Model' KM4Dev wiki   **http://wiki.km4dev.org/wiki/index.php/DIKW_model#KM4Dev_ Discussions** accessed 16 April 2012).
10   Nonaka, I. (1991), 'The knowledge creating company', *Harvard Business Review*, November–December, pp. 96–104.
11   Nonaka, I. and Takeuchi, N. (1995) *The Knowledge Creating Company*, Oxford University Press.
12   Davenport and Prusak (2000), p. 11.
13   This is said to be the weaker link in the knowledge spiral, as not all knowledge can be shared in this way, but some certainly can.
14   Snowden, D. (2010) 'Enabling an ecological model, preferably with intelligence' *KIM Legal* Dec 2010/Jan 2011, pp. 16–19.
15   Heuristics = simple efficient rules, which may be innate or learned, which

help people make decisions, but which sometimes lead to systematic errors. They include rules of thumb, intuitive judgements and common sense.

16 Zack, M. (2002) 'Developing a knowledge strategy' in Choo, C. and Bontis, N. (2002) *The Strategic Management of Intellectual Capital and Organizational Knowledge*, Oxford University Press, Oxford, pp. 255–76.

17 Spender, J. C. (1998) in Newell et al (2002) *Managing Knowledge Work*, Palgrave, Basingstoke.

18 Blackler, F. (1995) 'Knowledge, knowledge work and organizations: an overview and interpretation' *Organisation Studies* 16:6, 1021–46.

19 Kelleher, D. and Levene, S. (2001) *Knowledge Management: A Guide to Good Practice*, BSI.

20 Heisig, P. and Iske, P. (2003) 'European Guide to Good Practice in Knowledge Management: Final Draft for European Framework on Knowledge Management', via Chaffey, D. and Wood, S. *Business Information Management* Pearson Education Ltd, p. 228.

21 Benetton, L. (2011) 'Knowledge management know-how' *Lawyers Weekly* August 05.

Chapter 3

Personal knowledge management

After reading this chapter you will appreciate:

■ What personal knowledge management (PKM) is

■ How it can be used within a law firm:

    – as a foundation stone;
    – as a whole-firm strategy; and
    – as a supplement.

■ The tools, techniques and training needed for successful PKM systems

■ How you can use PKM for your own knowledge-building and career advancement

---

Personal knowledge management

Introduction

Personal knowledge management (PKM) is the practice where each individual is given the responsibility for managing their own knowledge, rather than their employer organising it for them.

This chapter looks at PKM from two points of view:

1. Firstly, as a system that law firms may want to use for technical legal work and/or support staff's knowledge:

    (a)   as a foundation stone for all KM work;
    (b)   as a supplement to broader systems; or
    (c)   as the main knowledge system.

2. Secondly, from the reader's perspective, as a way to support and build his/her own knowledge to further their career.

Although this chapter can stand alone, you may find it helpful to re-read it after you have finished the book, when your thoughts about top-down, firm-wide knowledge management systems are clearer.

What is PKM?

David Gurteen defines PKM in the following way:

> Personal knowledge management is taking responsibility for what you know, who you know – and what they know.[1]

PKM isn't business-wide, organised, imposed knowledge systems ('big KM'). PKM is an individually controlled process. It is about giving individuals the responsibility for and tools to manage their own information and knowledge. It is about helping individuals to develop their own personalised systems for learning and retrieval of useful information from external sources, their own way to store, evaluate and retrieve knowledge in a way that suits them. As explained by Frand and Hixon:[2]

> [PKM] provides a strategy for transforming what might be random pieces of information into something that can be systematically applied and that expands our personal knowledge.

Although not described as a model until fairly recently[3] PKM probably sounds familiar to most readers. Certainly when I undertook my training contract in 1996, although it wasn't called 'PKM', this was the method that I was expected to adopt in order to manage what I learned. My training contract was in a mid-sized regional firm specialising in dispute resolution. I was encouraged to develop my own system of files for precedents, checklists and 'useful information' from the first day of my training contract, to supplement both the library I had built up during my LPC year and the texts available from the firm in its law library and on its basic online systems. I kept anonymised copies of all court documents I drafted or admired, and constantly renewed them with updated versions as the court rules changed or as I found better versions. I kept extracts from advices which covered common issues and annotated them with my own reflections as to how successful or otherwise they were as I experienced successes and failures in different matters. It was an entirely paper-based system and a little ad hoc, but this was a form of PKM.

PKM as a whole-firm KM strategy

PKM can be used as a whole firm system, whereby no centralised effort is put into preparing precedents or central knowledge packs.

PKM is a simple and cheap system, but these aren't the main reasons that PKM is preferred by some businesses to big KM. The key benefit of PKM is that individuals add context as they filter, validate and understand what they read or learn: adding their own experiences to the knowledge they discover, making value-added knowledge for themselves and others.

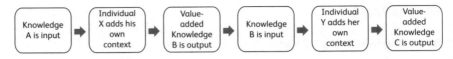

Figure 3.1 PKM: creation of value-added knowledge

It is often said that individual ad hoc methods of KM aren't as efficient as firm-wide, top-down, big KM, but in some situations PKM is actually more efficient, because the knowledge system adapts to the different learning levels and styles of the individual, becoming the ultimate tailored system. Professional work is often non-standard and when big KM standardises existing knowledge, something indefinable can be lost. That 'something' may be the tacit knowledge that really adds value to a client's work. Those trying to impose big KM in law firms find that it is difficult to force people to adopt or change work practices. PKM overcomes this problem by placing individuality at the heart of its system.

The key benefit of having PKM as a primary KM system within a firm is that it is a low-cost method that doesn't require a significant investment in technology and the attendant costs of training and effect on productivity caused by an upheaval in working practices. It is also by definition a highly personalised system, as each staff member chooses the way of managing their knowledge which suits them best, so when it is done well, it is very efficient and, some would say, suits the highly individual types who work in law firms. It places the knowledge creation and gathering within the hands of the experts themselves – the practitioners, whether they are fee earners or support staff. This also improves the motivation of staff to become involved, because the benefits of managing their knowledge in this way are so tangible, providing a personal benefit to them. However, reward systems will need to be adapted carefully, as this personal efficiency won't always naturally align with business needs: a law firm needs staff to do non-chargeable business development, not purely earn fees efficiently. Lastly, when combined with a sincere effort to connect staff, PKM means less time is spent trying to codify fee earners' tacit knowledge and more time is spent connecting people so that they can share their tacit knowledge through personal interactions.

There are a number of disadvantages to PKM. A primary issue for law firms is loss of knowledge when staff leave. Even though employment contracts could require staff to leave paper and digital files, these are likely to be so personalised that they would not be easy to share with remaining staff. This problem can be ameliorated by a sincere effort to connect people, such that each person's 'knowledge' is reflected on by others within the team who add their own value to that knowledge within the firm.

Another significant issue is the additional difficulty in senior staff recognising patterns of work and producing combined best practice. It is also difficult in a PKM system to enforce minimum quality standards and house style, which may affect brand and levels of professional negligence claims.

Also, PKM inevitably leads to a duplication of work, as, for example, everyone prepares their own workflows of varying quality for the same transaction type, when a single one, developed from a number of the best ones could be re-used by all. PKM proponents would argue, however, that value is added by each individual developing that workflow and that the individual nature of each brings a benefit. However, for easily commoditised work, PKM may not be the most efficient way of working within law firms.

Lastly, it is possible that if handled poorly, the focus on the 'self' could lead to weaker connections between staff and, importantly, there are security issues which will need to be addressed.

PKM as a whole-firm solution is unlikely to suit larger firms or those which want to commoditise their work and work with high leverage, but it may suit firms where work is non-standard and where there is less overlap between areas of work, where the problems of duplication and best practice are less important. Quality, consistency and house style must not be a particular concern, so it is likely to suit a firm where staff know and trust each other, and teams or departments are small.

The idea of a wholly personalised programme of KM may seem at odds with the accepted tenets of KM, especially because the knowledge won't be readily available for all to access. However, many knowledge managers have wasted time and resources trying to codify and store their staff's explicit and tacit knowledge with mixed results, both in relation to the quality of what is captured and the level to which this knowledge is accessed and leveraged by others later. People usually prefer dealing with people and prefer to speak to others to answer their questions rather than search a database; the more complex the answer they are looking for, such as the particularly knotty problems lawyers come across, the more likely they are to look to a personal discussion rather than at an information technology (IT) solution.

PKM can work as a whole-firm strategy in a very simple, inexpensive, non-technological way whereby fee earners are given responsibility for managing their own knowledge using paper files, and the firm concentrates on giving them the tools to extract and create knowledge, and manage it well (training ideas are listed below in this chapter). A firm could use online tools and social tagging for generic and non-confidential material.[4] Fee earners and support staff create their own workflows, knowledge banks, etc. that suit their own way of working and the firm would concentrate on creating excellent relationships between staff to enable knowledge-flow through face-to-face meetings, team meetings, networking and social meetings.

BOX 3.1   PKM at Xerox[5]

Jack Whalen, a sociologist, works at Xerox's Palo Alto Research Centre. A few years ago, he was assigned to the Institute for Research on Learning, a non profit group Xerox supported. He spent a couple of years there studying how people, computers, and expert-system software interacted in a customer service call centre in Lewisville, Texas, north of Dallas.

The software (in this case, Inference Corp.'s CasePoint) was supposed to help employees tell customers how to fix problems with copiers – paper jams, faded copies, and the like. When the call-centre operator typed in words spoken by a customer – 'jam' for example – the software searched its memory bank of diagnoses and solutions.

The trouble was that employees weren't using the new software. Management decided that employees needed an incentive to change. The company held a month-long contest in which employees earned points (which translated into cash) each time they solved a customer problem, by whatever means. The winner was an eight-year veteran named Carlos, with more than 900 points. Carlos wasn't a big favourite among managers – 'He's a cowboy', one of them said – but his victory was no surprise. He almost never used the software.

The runner up was a shock. Trish had been with the company just four months and had no previous experience with copying equipment. Her 600 points more than doubled the score of the third-place finisher. She didn't even have the new software, only an older, less sophisticated system. But she had a secret weapon: she sat across from Carlos. She overheard him when he talked. She apprenticed herself to him and persuaded him to show her the innards of copiers during lunch breaks. She built up a personal collection of manuals and handwritten notes about how to fix problems.

When designing a whole-firm PKM system such as this, it may help to think about the different aspects in the knowledge cycle: creation and discovery, evaluation, codification, storage, use, destruction and adaption. Staff will need training in all of these aspects, supported by quick guides and reference documents. They will probably also need time and administrative support to get their system set up and have either ongoing administrative support (reversing recent trends to lower fee earner-secretary ratios), or a lower chargeable time target to allow for time spent on PKM. They will need appropriate training and tools, as listed below.

One of the key aspects of PKM is management and retrieval, and some fee earners will need help in organising and arranging their systems. The aim is for each individual's system to be idiosyncratic and suit them personally, but fee earners can find it difficult to stop fee earning and invest sufficient time in creating these systems; to avoid quality issues, a firm will probably have to invest in assisting with this.

BOX 3.2 K-Profile

In his book *Know your value? Value what you know,*[6] Mike Cope, a consultant in this field, has developed a methodology for assessing and managing personal capital, made up of knowledge stock, knowledge currency and knowledge flow.

Knowledge stock is how your knowledge is stored and what type of knowledge it is (e.g. explicit or tacit).

Knowledge currency is the way that we acquire and share knowledge, whether by head (thinking), hand (observable behaviours, responses, reactions), or heart (emotional skills to connect, build trust and collaborate).

Knowledge flow is the processes for knowledge: discovery, delay (storage for later use), dispose, diffuse (knowledge-sharing) and deliver (capitalising and getting a pay-back for your knowledge).

By studying these aspects and putting them into a table such as Table 3.1 below, you can map out existing knowledge, see gaps and determine how you intend to fill those gaps and what strategies would work best.

Table 3.1 Summary of the explicit and tacit aspects of knowledge flow

	Discover	Delay	Dispose	Diffuse	Deliver
Explicit (head)	Explore new codified knowledge	Store codified knowledge	Discard old codified knowledge	Share codified knowledge	Sell codified knowledge
Tacit (heart or hand)	Acquire new intuitive knowledge	Store intuitive knowledge for later use	Discard old intuitive knowledge	Share intuitive knowledge	Sell intuitive knowledge

Source: From *The Complete Idiot's Guide to Knowledge Management*, by Melissie Clemmons Rumizen (2002) CWL Publishing Enterprises. Used by permission of Alpha Books, an imprint of Penguin Group (USA) Inc. © 1998 Alpha Books.

PKM as a supplemental system

Even those firms which wish to invest in top-down, big KM may find it helpful to retain PKM as a strategy for some departments or to fill gaps in what they are able to afford. Departments where there are few employees or where the cost is not justified by the return on investment, usually where work is difficult to standardise or commoditise, may suit PKM as a supplemental system. Some examples may be a sole practitioner in a field, a support department, and the KM aspect of a professional support lawyer's work.

In this situation a firm will need to target the training tools and techniques on a smaller group. The key is to make this an explicit, clear part of overall strategy and for individuals to understand what is expected and why, and to be supported in that.

PKM as a foundation stone

Whatever a firm's broader KM system, PKM can act as a useful foundation stone on which the rest of the KM strategy is built. PKM systems emphasise individuals' responsibility for knowledge gathering and sharing, and providing the tools for it, which are useful in all KM systems. Also, no matter how the value of sharing knowledge is emphasised, there will always be some resistant elements for whom the value of enforcing a top-down, big KM strategy is not off-set by its cost. These can be the most diligent and organised lawyers or those for whom a paper rather than online collection is far more user-friendly, and therefore efficient, at giving them the knowledge that they need. If a firm has included PKM teachings as part of its overall strategy, this can act as a safety net for those unable to join in with using the main KM systems and also help individuals with knowledge capture and analysis, even if this is later kept on a centralised database.

When using PKM as a foundation stone, a firm will need to include the majority of the training listed below and extract whichever of the tools and techniques listed are relevant to it.

PKM tools, techniques and skills

In designing their own personalised systems, individuals may want to begin by using the K-Profile method explained in Box 3.2 above, which will help them to understand in a systematic way what they already know and where there are gaps in their knowledge and to devise strategies to fill those gaps.

To make any PKM system work, a business will need to provide appropriate skills and training, which are more easily considered under the following headings:[7]

1. **Strategy** – staff will need to understand why knowledge is being managed in this way: the benefits and risks. They will need to understand what they need to manage and why, and develop their own strategy. Without this, it is unlikely to become a habit.
2. **Retrieving information** – there is a massive amount of information available. Staff will need to have regular training on the most efficient way to retrieve the information that they need, including training in internet search, Boolean logic, and training in the importance of keeping their knowledge current. Staff will also need to come to an understanding of their own level of expertise and be honest with themselves

about the level of technical training they need. A firm will need to provide their usual law library and any externally provided systems, such as LexisNexisButterworths (LNB) and Practical Law Company (PLC).[8] A firm would probably also want to include within this heading training in speed reading and analysis skills, a listening skills course, refresher legal research skills courses, IT and internet search training as well as ongoing training (not just induction training) in any externally provided systems which are used. Staff will need to be confident about using aggregators, feed readers and social bookmarks. They will need to develop their own taxonomy (also known as a folksonomy).

3. **Evaluating and analysing information** – just as law students need to be taught to understand the hierarchy of authority for legal information and its level of authority within court proceedings (All ER reports before WLR, primary sources before secondary, etc.) all staff will need training to understand and question the authority of information (primary sources, blogs of known experts, comments by unknown people). As well as judging the quality of information, staff will need to judge its relevance to their practice and/or the particular issue at hand. Staff will need to understand how to validate information and be encouraged to question and form tentative opinions, perhaps by writing blog posts and podcasts, 'What I learned' articles, learning diaries and 'after action learning' schemes.[9] They should also be able to write articles for publication and prepare seminars. Staff will need to understand how to filter out the noise based on personal criteria.

4. **Managing and organising information and ideas** – staff will need to be given access to ways of managing their information and be given regular updated training in the most efficient ways of managing this. This could be low tech, such as paper files and folders, or higher tech, such as online social bookmarking systems, or a document management system (DMS). Staff will also need to be taught the means to analyse data, to synthesise information and describe patterns, trends and flows, perhaps using wikis, mind maps or spreadsheets. They will have to learn in simple terms how to be their own librarians, developing their own categorisations. Importantly, they will also need to understand when it is appropriate to delete or destroy information, or the system will become too unwieldy. This training should also include advice about security aspects, confidentiality, client privacy and data protection. It should also cover personal effectiveness: working as a team with their support staff, utilising relevant technology to leverage their business tools and customising their environment (computer and physical workstation) to maximise their effectiveness. Individuals will need to make their information collections understandable and quick and easy to access, with a logical presentation which suits them personally. They will need access to calendar and diary systems, and to develop their own to-do lists and workflows.

5. **Collaboration** – if the firm is to make the most of its fee earners in a PKM system, it must encourage collaboration by staff. Again, this can be by high tech methods, such as groupware tools like SharePoint and tools for virtual meetings, but can also be low tech, such as professional groups, personal networking groups, knowledge sharing meetings, etc. Staff may also find Twitter and joining Tweetchats useful; instant messaging, video conferencing, and of course emails and telephone.

PKM for personal growth

This section is written to help you, the reader, help yourself in managing your own knowledge for your career. It is a given these days that you are unlikely to have a job for life, so how can you manage your own personal knowledge to maximise your own expertise?

If you are a professional support lawyer, knowledge lawyer or other professional, you may find that whilst you are an expert in your original field of specialism, you may struggle with the KM aspects of your work. Unless you work for a very large firm, you will probably not have systems in place to help you learn about and keep up to date about KM itself, so these PKM tools and techniques will hopefully assist you.

When developing your personal PKM strategy, concentrate on two aspects: informing yourself and connecting yourself.

Informing yourself

In relation to informing yourself, please re-read the previous sections on whole firm PKM strategy with your own work in mind and arrange a system to suit you. You will need to invest time in this for it to work, but if you can see it as an investment in your career, hopefully you will be able to prioritise it.

Investigate different means of aggregating relevant and useful information to find the means that suits you best. Train yourself: re-read the skills training list above and arrange some training. Remember to apply the evaluation tests to the knowledge you discover. (What is the source of this information? How expert is this commentator? How trustworthy is this information?)

You may also want to apply the K-Profile system to your own knowledge and perhaps use the opportunity to develop your own private web pages with montages of information in different media, which will not only be useful for the future, but teach you some practical IT skills.

Connecting yourself

In connecting yourself, see Annex 3A below for some top tips for connecting yourself to others in your field, especially useful if you are a lone expert in your firm. Tell your stories to your new connections. Your personal knowledge is unique and valuable. You will be surprised at how you can help others with it and, as many lawyers discover, when you become a trusted source, you can begin to wield influence on those around you, so begin by giving without expecting to receive and you will develop influence.

In connecting yourself look widely at alumni groups, at clubs and local interest groups, as well as professional associations, communities of practice and internet groups. Diversity is important as it sparks creativity in looking at problems from different angles and opens opportunities which you wouldn't otherwise have found. If your budget can afford it, try to attend a conference that isn't squarely in your field of expertise, but one that looks cutting edge or fascinating to you. Spending time with creative productive people is rarely wasted. If they work in a different sector they will have a new perspective on your problems and perhaps help you with innovative solutions.

Summary: the least you should know

■ PKM places the responsibility for managing an individual's knowledge-needs within his/her own hands and gives him/her the tools to do that.

■ PKM can be used within a law firm as:

  – a foundation stone – suitable for all firms;
  – a whole-firm strategy – suitable for smaller or niche firms where staff are well-connected, stable and where work is highly individual and unlikely to benefit from commoditisation;
  – a supplement – to fill in gaps in big KM.

■ Staff will need training in knowledge management retrieval, evaluation and management, to be encouraged in collaboration and will need to be supported with the right tools.

■ All the techniques described in this chapter can be used by you, the reader, to further your career and you are encouraged to concentrate on connecting and informing yourself.

ANNEX 3A: Top tips for connecting yourself to people

1. **Give to get** – when you connect people to other people or the information/ knowledge that they need, you become a 'trusted source', just like the ideal 'trusted adviser' every lawyer wants to become, which increases your ability to influence and encourages reciprocation. When networking, concentrate on how you can help others. The less you think about the return you are looking for, the greater that return in the long run.
2. **Use ready-made groups** – build a diverse portfolio of networking groups, with a mix of groups based on professional expertise (Association of Litigation PSLs), geo-graphically based professional groups (local law society, local Gurteen Knowledge group) and mixed background groups (alumni, clubs, local interest groups). Diversity sparks creativity and helps you understand what you didn't realise you didn't know.
3. **Be prepared** – before you go anywhere, get a copy of the list of attendees and see if there is anyone you particularly want to meet or if there are any particular work issues you would like to discuss. Often, having a plan and a couple of goals to fulfil makes introducing yourself to others and starting conversations easier.
4. **Pay attention** – most people are happy to discuss themselves and their work if you listen and pay attention to their non-verbal clues.
5. **Keep in touch with people** – the internet provides many varied ways of staying in touch with those who are no longer within your personal face-to-face network; just make sure that you use the right tool for the right group – LinkedIn is appropriate for professional networks but Facebook may be more suitable for personal relation-ships.
6. **Act as host or get involved** – if you find the social aspect of networking a struggle, you may find it easier to be the host or take on a defined role, such as club secretary. This is often less work than you would imagine, and as you will have a defined job to do and a good reason to chat to everyone as you greet them and check that they are enjoying the event, the social aspect becomes easier than simply starting conversa-tions with strangers.

Endnotes

1 Gurteen, D. **www.gurteen.com/gurteen/gurteen.nsf/id/pkm** (accessed 5 April 2012).
2 Frand, J. And Hixon, C. (1999) *Personal Knowledge Management: Who, What, Why, When, Where, How?* (**www.anderson.ucla.edu/faculty/jason.frand/ researcher/speeches/PKM.htm**) p. 1 (accessed 12 April 2012).
3 Ibid.
4 These change with such frequency that no recommendations can be made, but something similar to Digg or delicious would work well (see glossary, Appendix 1).
5 Parsons, M., (2004) *Effective Knowledge Management for Law Firms*, Oxford University Press, pp. 174–5.
6 Cope, M. (2000) *Know your value? – Value what you know*, Financial Times Management.

7 Adapted from Prof Paul Dorsey's framework developed at Milikin University, as discussed by Barth, S. (2003) 'Personal Toolkit: A framework for PKM tools' *KM World* 1 January **www.kmworld.com/Articles/Editorial/Feature/Personal-toolkit-A-framework-for-personal-knowledge-management-tools-9416.aspx** (accessed 12 April 2012).
8 Organisations which provide legal content, analysis and know-how for their subscribers.
9 See Chapter 6 and Chapter 7, Box 7.1.

Chapter 4

Strategies

This chapter covers the following:

- why a KM strategy is a good idea for your firm
- why it should be aligned to your business strategy and how to do this
- when a departmental KM strategy will be useful
- how to start writing a firm or departmental strategy
- the process you could use to design and implement a KM strategy
- the best KM strategies are constantly evolving

Why should you have a KM strategy?

Law firms instinctively 'do' knowledge management (KM) because they are knowledge businesses. Similarly, whether you realise it or not, your firm already has a KM strategy, if only an implicit one.

An implicit KM strategy reflects your firm's culture and mode of working. Your firm's particular culture – collaborative/sharing, eat-what-you-kill – is reflected in how it chooses staff, offices and work methods. Your firm will provide its lawyers with a library and some knowledge resources, some precedents, templates or checklists to make work easier. Your firm may encourage fee earners to keep their own files of precedents and useful information, or it may encourage its fee earners to keep these centrally for everyone to access. It also trains and rewards its lawyers in a manner which perpetuates its culture. These attributes combine to form your firm's implicit knowledge strategy.

If you have no explicit KM strategy for your firm, it may seem like an immense task to develop one, but it will be worthwhile. Your firm's existing implicit knowledge strategy is unlikely to be the most effective way to promote your firm's best interests or reflect where the firm wishes to go. A fully thought-out, explicit strategy will assist your firm by helping everyone working within the firm to focus knowledge resources on the most strategically important aspects, helping to minimise any wastes of time and resources and focusing efforts on the areas of knowledge work with the highest pay-off. Secondly, a written KM strategy will help everyone within your firm understand what that strategy is, improving engagement and helping you mobilise support. It helps to justify expenditure of time and money and helps the firm speak a common language. Lastly, a written strategy will help your implementation plans to stay on track, providing a clear framework for action, avoiding anyone being tempted into inefficient expenditure.

There is a major risk in writing strategies, especially in professional services firms: that the process of strategising becomes an end in itself and valuable time for improvement can be lost whilst the perfect document is researched, analysed, defined and refined. A perfect strategy is extremely useful, but why waste any time in implementing good practice whilst you produce this perfect document? Why not start by making your firm more efficient, cutting costs and being more profitable straight away by using 'fast-track mini-strategies'? By comparing existing KM activity against business strategy, you are half way to a useful strategy in any event. A mini-strategy can be written in less than four weeks and should set out very briefly what is currently being done, how it compares against existing business strategy, identifying any existing good practices to be continued and extended, and identifying any obvious quick wins to act on immediately. A mini-strategy can take any shape and use any format, but for an example to help you, see Annex 4A.

In fact, make yourself a coffee and take ten minutes *right now* to look at Annex 4A and jot down some notes to mull over whilst reading the rest of this book. Don't be cynical about this: just do it. As David Maister says[1] regarding whole-firm business strategies 'Try something, anything, but act – *now*!' If something doesn't work, change it, but don't waste the opportunity to improve practices straight away.

What should your KM strategy encompass?

Once you have your fast-track mini-strategy up and running, you will need to turn your attention to your full KM Strategy.

You should first consider what kind of strategy you should develop and where you should focus your attention to get the greatest return on investment.

There are many academic theories about 'KM strategies' and which kinds of strategies are the most effective (see Box 4.1).

BOX 4.1   KM strategy types

Knowledge strategy as business strategy

These strategies:

- are comprehensive;
- emphasise knowledge creation, capture, organisation, renewal, sharing and use;
- aim to have available and use the best possible knowledge at each point of action within the firm;
- see knowledge as a 'product';
- are often used in law firms.

Personal knowledge asset responsibility strategy

These strategies:

- emphasise personal responsibility for knowledge, encouraging individuals to manage and share their knowledge;
- are often the default implicit strategy in law firms.

Knowledge creation strategy

These strategies:

- emphasise innovation and creation of new knowledge through organisational learning, basic and applied research and development;
- motivate employees to innovate and capture lessons learned for the purpose of obtaining new and better knowledge to lead to improved competitiveness;
- tend to be the strategies adopted by market leaders and those shaping the future of a particular niche market.

Knowledge transfer strategy

These strategies

- emphasise systematic approaches to transfer of knowledge and best practices in order to improve operational efficiency and quality.

Customer-focused knowledge strategy

These strategies:

- aim to understand customers and their needs in detail in order to improve market offerings and customer care at each level of service.

Intellectual asset management strategy

These strategies:

- are less relevant to law firms;

42

> - concentrate on exploiting existing assets and emphasise management of patents, technologies, operational and management practices, customer relations, organisational arrangements, and other structural knowledge assets;
> - concentrate on renewing, organising, evaluating, safekeeping, as well as increasing the availability and marketing of these assets.

Whilst in whole-business strategies business leaders are advised to concentrate on customer, price or product, in relation to KM strategies, the most efficient strategies are a mix of the strategic aims in Box 4.1, with the actual proportions dependent on the business in question.

In developing your KM strategy, start by studying the needs of your business and the particular challenges it faces. Ask yourself how your sector is changing and what your competitors are doing to differentiate themselves. You may want to follow their example, or use this information to carve out a slightly different niche for yourself. Every business is slightly different and requires slightly different solutions to knowledge challenges. You will find more detail and suggested lists of questions later on in this chapter.

Obviously firms would like to excel at everything, but this is unrealistic. Successful firms are those that take every aspect into account, but focus actions on a few primary goals, the ones which will bring that particular firm the best strategic advantage in its own particular market, with its own particular mix of staff, technology and work practices.

Getting mobilised: what process should you use?

The processes involved for a fast-track mini-strategy, a detailed departmental strategy and a firm-wide detailed KM strategy are all very different.

Fast-track mini KM strategy

A fast-track mini-strategy can be developed by one knowledgeable and enthusiastic person who has studied the firm's business strategy and spoken to a few key front-line staff. It can be developed quickly (i.e. within four weeks) and begin the strategic focus early on in the process whilst the firm develops a more detailed KM strategy.

Your firm's first firm-wide strategy

Before you begin planning the process for developing your strategy, you will need to decide who should have ultimate responsibility for it. Whilst it is important that many voices are heard during the process, you will need to identify someone senior to head up the project, with the authority to drive things forward. In a large firm this may be a KM Director or Head of Knowledge. In smaller firms, it is likely to be a senior partner leading the project, with support from one or more senior associates.

BOX 4.2   Top tip

You may assume your firm's managing partner or chief executive is the right person to be the project sponsor, but this is rarely so.
   When choosing the appropriate person, look for someone who:

- commands respect;
- whilst not necessarily an expert, is someone who understands the point of KM;
- has enthusiasm, drive and the time needed to get things done;
- has excellent communication skills: KM can seem a nebulous concept, difficult to explain, and someone will have to make the staff understand why this extra work will be worthwhile.

Once you have your project sponsor, he or she can decide who is suitable for the role of project leader, who then decides what kind of support they need. The project leader will need to take soundings from a wide-variety of staff during the process, but will need a small team to work directly with them. Teams larger than three people can be unwieldy in a project of this nature, but how large the direct report group needs to be will depend on the level of work needed and the existing commitments of staff. The team will need to agree governance issues (who reports what to whom, when) but this can be done informally.

After the project sponsor, project leader and project team have been identified, you will need to decide what process you want to use to develop the strategy document. The process will depend on the amount of work which needs to be done, but if this is a first KM strategy, the process will probably look similar to that in Figure 4.1.

To balance top-down and bottom-up consultation, you should:

1. Identify the key staff groups within the organisation. These groups deliver the greatest business value, or are involved in the most important business activities.
2. Conduct comprehensive and holistic needs analysis activities with selected staff groups, to identify key needs and issues.
3. Supplement this research with input from senior management and organisational strategy documents, to determine an overall strategic focus.
4. Based on these findings, develop recommendations for addressing the issues and needs identified.

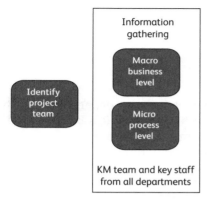

Figure 4.1: Knowledge management strategy process

5. Implement a series of strategic and tactical initiatives, based on the recommendations. These will select suitable KM techniques and approaches.

There is debate about the benefits of top-down and bottom-up approaches to information gathering and consultation, but the best solution is to have a mix of both.

You will need top-down inputs to capture the business's key strategic plans, some of which may be sensitive. You will also need top-down input from the finance departments, which again may include sensitive information. If your firm doesn't tend to distribute information widely amongst its workforce, you may need to be prepared from an early stage to create two versions of your KM strategy document, one including finances and sensitive information and a second, shorter, version without.

The difficulty with purely top-down strategies, even if they are extremely well researched, creative and soundly argued, is that you still have to take the strategy to departments and persuade them that changes to their mode of operation are worthwhile. Most partners value their independence and are confident in their modes of work, and cannot be 'told' to change, only persuaded. It is much easier to start with the front-line workers and create a strategy in consultation with them, focused on the way that they work, with a clear eye on improving their working practices to make them more efficient and their work more enjoyable. The difficulty with bottom-up input is that it can get unwieldy very quickly, so you will have to manage the process ruthlessly.

Whoever you consult, remember to leave sufficient time between meetings and release dates for detailed comments to come in. A large proportion of lawyers prefer to mull over information from a meeting then reach their conclusions, rather than give a snap judgement at a meeting, perhaps because most are Myers-Briggs INTJ (Intuitive, Introverts, Thinkers, Judgers) personality types.[2]

For a departmental strategy

If your firm is sufficiently large to warrant separate departmental KM strategies, it is probably large enough to have whole firm business and departmental strategies, so writing a departmental KM strategy is a process of looking at what is currently done in the field of KM and how it fits with business objectives, looking for gaps, writing a draft, then consulting partners in the department and others to finalise it.

You can easily use the existing business strategy template for the KM strategy, with a few changes.

If you do not have a departmental business strategy, developing a KM strategy will be more complex. You will need to tease out from partners what the aims of the department are over the coming five years. It may not be written down, but departmental leads will have an idea how they are concentrating their efforts to build the business: through specialisation, commoditisation for more clients, fewer but better served quality clients, merger-growth, and lateral hires, etc. Once this is clarified, you can follow the questions and processes above, adapted for a departmental strategy.

Gathering the information

How you gather the information for your strategy is almost as important as the list of questions that need answering. All KM strategies require cultural change to some degree, so you will need to keep staff on your side as far as possible and minimise future change management problems.

Initially you will need to explain why the information needs to be gathered, so a short programme of presentations may be needed, depending on the level of awareness of KM matters within your firm. It is important to avoid personnel misunderstanding the information-gathering process and becoming defensive because they think this is part of a performance review process.

Once staff understand the reason for your information gathering, decide how you want to go about it. There are a number of ways in which you could approach the information-gathering process. Use whichever suits you and your firm best. It is probably best to use more than one technique for a more complete view. Different techniques will work for different groups, so stay flexible. You might want to consider facilitated discussions, focus groups, surveys, staff interviews, workplace observation, contextual inquiry and task analysis. You could have a series of meetings, either ad hoc or a formal programme, or a planning day. Meetings are more flexible and responsive to need and a programme which is spread over time probably suits lawyers' personality types better, but a planning day focuses everyone's minds and leads to quicker solutions.

You may find it helpful to divide your detailed investigations into a macro-level investigation into the firm's business strategy and a micro-level investigation into each department's needs and ask questions about staff, processes and clients. You need to find out what your firm is doing, why it is doing it, if/how it meets business objectives, what benefits accrue and how these benefits are measured.

You may want to divide information gathering down departmental lines, as KM solutions in one department are likely to differ from those in another. Within those departments, it may be useful to use the six disciplines of information search and management, workflows, collaboration, training and learning, networking and client-facing knowledge services.[3]

Try to leave solutions aside at the beginning and leave benchmarking to the end of the process. Start with the business needs and fit the solution (which may or may not be a technological solution) to the needs.

BOX 4.3   Business needs

1. Staffing

(a) Are you hiring the right calibre of people for your market niche? If not, do your work practices put staff (lawyers or support staff) off?

(b) Are your staff better trained than your competitors? Are they particularly skilled and valuable to a particular niche in the market?

(c) Do your staff have appropriate opportunities for networking and knowledge-sharing, out of which emerge new ideas?

(d) Are your staff happy in their work or do they express frustrations at working practices?

2. Processes

(a) Are you happy with levels of non-chargeable time?

(b) Are you happy with levels of written-off time?

(c) Are you happy with levels of professional indemnity claims?

(d) How do your staff think their work could be made more efficient? How would they like to cut out repetitive tasks?

3. Clients

(a) Do you have adequate information about your clients' needs?

(b) Do you invest in research and development on issues of particular interest to your clients?

Once you are happy that you understand the needs of your business, you need to ask how KM techniques can help you achieve these aims. If you are uncertain whether an activity is a 'KM activity', ask yourself whether knowledge is being learnt, retrieved, used, shared or stored: if that process uses knowledge in any of these ways, KM techniques may help improve efficiency.

In considering how KM can help the firm achieve its aims, it is often useful to check that the basics are covered in all departments under each of the six disciplines and to prioritise these basics, before looking beyond to more advanced KM activities.

As regards a macro-level investigation of business strategy, if you have nothing written down, you will need to look at the culture, incentives, business benefit, roles and responsibilities of your firm. What sort of firm is yours? What sort of firm do you wish it to be? Look at how the firm is divided, what the attitude is to investment, and what the politics, power and leadership are like.

1. Do you have the basics covered?

    (a) Are you happy that your lawyers follow best practice, use the right precedents and adhere to your house-style?
    (b) Are your lawyers up to date with the basic legal knowledge needed for their work?
    (c) Are there efficient, easy-to-use ways for your fee earners to access and analyse existing explicit knowledge in their daily work?
    (d) Do you make the most of the existing knowledge for marketing purposes? Knowledge can be re-used in internal training, firm e-zines/newsletters, external publishing, and client seminars.

2. Do your fee earners have the opportunity to go beyond the basics?

    (a) Does your firm provide opportunities for networking and discussing work, both to solve existing work problems and also for innovation and creativity or specialist learning?
    (b) Do your fee earners have the opportunity to develop new knowledge?
    (c) Are your fee earners well-connected?
    (d) Do your fee earners know who is an expert in what?
    (e) Are there opportunities for tacit knowledge to be passed between fee earners?
    (f) Do you retain knowledge? Do you have any succession plans? Do you recover the knowledge created by your fee earners in their work for re-use by other fee earners and also for retention within the firm once those fee earners have left?

3. What systems will you use?

    (a) What technologies do you already have?

(b)   What technologies do you think you need?

(c)   Can you leverage the technology you currently have? Sometimes systems used for support functions can be used for knowledge sharing by fee earners.

4.   What budget do you have for any future changes? Remember that budgets for KM plans such as these may currently be included in different pots (i.e. marketing, training, departmental budgets).

5.   In the light of your discoveries, where does your firm want to focus its efforts: quality, consistency, sharing accessibility, community building, knowledge capture, minimising knowledge loss, learning and development, innovation, client relationships, better systems and efficiency in process?

Chapters 3, 5 and 6 in particular will help you prioritise your KM ideas, remembering that once the basics are codified, you will probably get the greatest return on investment by concentrating on tacit knowledge and connecting your staff and encouraging collaboration.

For example, your firm plans to develop expertise in a particular niche market, because it has investigated and identified a gap in a market related to one in which it already has an existing reputation. Your KM strategy to support this may include some of the following.

Information management and search and workflows

- **Basics** – Are you happy with house-style and basic precedents? Is there anything that needs to be put in place to ensure you comply with professional rules?
- **Beyond the basics** – Development of knowledge packs, detailed precedents and workflows in the new field by specialist lawyers as they develop their own expertise, to enable existing knowledge to be reused and for work to be leveraged beyond the specialist team as market share grows.
- **How? Budget?** – You could use new software for an online solution if you have the budget, or you could leverage software you already have, or, if the fee earners are in the same office, your solution could be paper-based.

Collaboration, training and learning

- **Basics** – Do any of your fee earners need basic training in this field to reach basic standards?
- **Beyond the basics** – Monthly internal training sessions by those lawyers who are specialising in this niche area to a wider group within the

firm to disseminate the knowledge they are developing and provide opportunities to collaborate on new ideas.

- **How? Budget?** – You may need to consider external training courses for the basics. Beyond the basics, if the fee earners are in the same office, face-to-face meetings would be ideal for collaboration and learning. If fee earners are in separate offices, an online collaboration tool may be useful.

Client-facing knowledge management

- **Basics** – Do you have an in-house newsletter on this topic, publicised on your website?
- **Beyond the basics** – Can you introduce new knowledge-based market-ing to this niche market, reusing the ideas developed in training and collaboration sessions, developing articles for various sources?
- **How? Budget?** – Anything written by your fee earners can be re-focused for external publishing, in-house e-zines, firm blogs or Face-book page, advertised on Twitter, developed into client seminar pro-grammes and/or client extranets.

Writing the strategy

How you set out your KM strategy is a matter for you. If you begin by concentrating on the 'what' and 'why' then the 'how' will follow in a focused way.

At the very least a KM strategy should set out who is doing what, when, where, how, why and how much it will cost. It should also resonate with your business leaders, as they will need to understand the strategy to implement it, inspire their staff and enforce adherence. However you set out the document, it needs to be a format that you can re-read and refer to easily. Box 4.4 has a list of elements that you will probably want to include, whatever format you use.

Whilst the format doesn't matter for the strategy document, be conscien-tious about spelling and grammar. You don't want fee earners to either be distracted from the content by mistakes or for them to assume the strategy is poor because the presentation is poor.

BOX 4.4   Elements to include

Objectives

- Analysis of the business background and objectives driving the KM objectives.

Approach

■ The vision for KM within the organisation.

Plan

■ The scope and boundaries of the plan – KM can creep into all aspects of running a law firm.
■ Implementation plan – its framework.
■ Lists of pilot programmes and evaluation plans (while accepting that you will never find perfect solutions, use pilots to weed out bad ideas, not perfect good ones).
■ Your must-haves and nice-to-haves.
■ Analyses (whichever helps your business):

  – SWOT (strengths, weaknesses, opportunities and threats);
  – PEST (political, environmental, social and technical);
  – Scenario analysis;
  – Porter's 5 forces;[4]
  – Porter's generic strategies.[5]

■ Your quick wins and long battles – use the covering fire of quick wins to make progress in the longer battles.
■ Have SMART goals (specific, measurable, agreed, realistic and time-related).
■ Make sure tools and techniques are matched to needs.
■ Prioritise goals.

Budget

■ Resources available and timescales.

Cost–benefit analysis

■ Review of the risks of implementation and risks to implementation.

Change management plans

■ Existing culture and any culture change plans.
■ Communication strategy.
■ Plan some quick wins to boost publicity.

Measurement systems

■ Outline of the measurement systems to be used.
■ Targets to be achieved – what 'success' and 'failure' will look like.

Appendices

■ A short 'roadmap' for easy reference.
■ A list of timescales for checking on progress and reviewing the strategy document itself to make sure your KM strategy is still aligned to business needs throughout the year as needs change.

Once a draft is written and ready for consultation, it needs to be available as a printable document, not just a web page or presentation. Most lawyers like to print off documents and read them quietly, write notes and process them over time, not glance at a web page. You will get the best feedback during your consultation, and hence the best implementation support later on, if you support staff during the consultation process.

Using the strategy

Lastly, once the strategy is finished, it is tempting to file it, but keep it to hand and keep it under review. Diarise regular reviews to check that it still meets business needs, as these will change over the year. Check regularly what is going well, what isn't and why it isn't and keep a note of what has worked well and what has been a struggle, and use this information to improve implementation next time. You should reach for your strategy whenever someone proposes increasing the scope of your responsibilities, introduces a new plan which affects the existing KM activity or wants to change business processes.

Use your strategy to pitch for support, to gain stakeholder support across board level, to keep you on track and avoid getting diverted from the most efficient way of using your budget by persuasive and influential partners.

Summary: the least you need to know

- A KM strategy is useful to focus resources on projects which give the greatest return, focus attention on KM and keep implementation plans on track.
- Your KM strategy ought to be aligned to your business strategy to focus resources.
- If you are unsure where to start in designing a KM strategy, begin with a short-form strategy, to begin improving focus straightaway, then gradually develop a wider, more detailed strategy. At the least, a strategy only needs to state where the firm is now in relation to KM, where it wants to be and the steps it needs to take to get there.
- The best KM strategies are constantly evolving: keep your strategy to hand, refer to it regularly and keep it under review.

ANNEX 4A: Fast-track short-form KM strategy

1.   What are your business's top three key objectives over the next five years?
2.   How do current knowledge activities support these objectives within each team or department?
3.   What budget and manpower do you have available for existing KM work and future projects?
4.   What simple changes can you make to fill gaps in KM support for business objectives? How can you leverage existing systems to fulfil KM needs?
5.   What large-scale changes to KM may be needed to fulfil these business objectives? What will you need to know in order to analyse possible solutions?

ANNEX 4B: Knowledge management strategies – a five-step practical guide

Depending on the nature and size of your firm, you may need to establish a representative steering group to consider the following points, and then pass the initial document through a review/approval group before finalising it. Your finalised KM strategy document may include an implementation plan and business plan.

Set out the strategy document in whatever way suits you and your firm best, but you will probably want to consider the following points:

1.   **Clarify business objectives:**

   •   What are your firm's official objectives? If nothing is published, it may help to consider your firm's implicit objectives under the following headings:
       –   Financial plan
       –   Growth plan
       –   Assets (people, knowledge, technology, etc.)
       –   Market sectors
       –   Demand profile (who is demanding your services and does your capacity match demand?)
       –   Brand
       –   Culture.
   •   Gather input in a structured manner from key staff, clients and comparable organisations, regarding their focus in the coming year.
   •   Use an appropriate analytical technique if it assists understanding and communication with others, such as SWOT (strengths, weaknesses, opportunities, threats); PEST (political, economic, social, technological); or heatmap.

2.   **Assess your current level of knowledge activity and your resources:**

   •   Review what you currently do in relation to KM, how and why. Do not spend time on a detailed knowledge audit at this stage, although this could be an objective for the coming period.
   •   Understand your current level of activity against comparable organisations

and whether there is a maturity gap. This is for background information: your KM strategy supports your business's strategy, not theirs.

3. **Ask how your knowledge activity currently supports your business objectives:**

   - Evaluate the effectiveness of your current programme of everyday work and projects.
   - Realign and refocus your knowledge activity to meet your business objectives.
   - Where needs are being met, review whether knowledge activity could be undertaken more effectively and efficiently.
   - Don't be afraid to sideline activities which are no longer meeting your business's objectives.
   - Identify gaps and then assess the cost against return of options to fill those gaps.

4. **Think about where you would ideally like to be in one, three and five years' time in relation to knowledge activity.**

5. **Make your strategy practical:**

   - Make your strategy a living document that you refer to regularly and adjust as required. If your strategy must be in a particular style for your Executive Board, consider having an additional short, plain English 'roadmap' for everyday use.
   - Make objectives SMART (specific, measureable, achievable, realistic and time-related) and keep them simple.
   - Prepare a mini-business case for each change you wish to make, measure current performance, apply the change then re-measure performance to assess its success. Avoid rolling out too many changes at the same time or you will lose the source of the improvements.
   - When considering changes:
     - prioritise any quick wins and leverage any technology you already have;
     - don't waste precious resources on practice areas/partners that work well without knowledge support: this can wait for more profitable times;
     - don't put off an important task looking for the perfect solution: implement a good 'work in progress' for the time being.

Once the strategy is written, try to refer to it whenever you start or complete a project, are asked to broaden your workload, or review your budget/departmental spend, so that you can keep your objectives in mind and focus on those tasks which promote your strategy. Establish a KM strategy review schedule, depending upon your objectives and the changing economic landscape. The KM strategy can provide the vision, but as the world changes, you will need to adapt your implementation programme.

Lastly, if you cannot find the time to write your strategy, write a short one-page 'roadmap' or a rough draft. Something will be better than nothing. In its simplest form, your strategy just needs to say where you are now, where you want to go and how you are going to get there.

Endnotes

1 Maister, D. (2003) *Managing the Professional Service Firm*, Simon & Schuster UK Ltd, p. 240.
2 If you are interested in the research into lawyers' personality types, see Russell, H. (2007) 'The power of personality' *KIM Legal* 16 October, 2:2. See also Chapter 7, 'Training and learning'.
3 See Chapter 2, 'What is knowledge'.
4 Porter, M.E. (1980) *Competitive Strategy: Techniques for Analyzing Industries and Competitors*, Free Press.
5 Porter, M.E. (1985) *Competitive Advantage: Creating and Sustaining Superior Performance*, Free Press.

Chapter 5

Codification and managing explicit knowledge

This chapter covers the following:

■ Ideas for managing the more easily codified aspects of fee earners' work

    – Workflows and case management
    – Precedents
    – Knowledge databases
    – Intranets

■ Improving a firm's knowledge-sharing culture

■ How to develop a knowledge map

■ Ideas to avoid the most common pitfalls in codification and management of explicit knowledge

---

Introduction

This chapter concerns codification. This is often the most appropriate means of managing explicit knowledge, but can relate to some tacit knowledge as well.

As discussed in Chapter 2, explicit knowledge is best summarised as:

• knowledge that is easy to share in words or writing;
• objective knowledge, which lends itself to rules and definitions;
• the easiest knowledge to capture, store and transmit electronically, i.e. put into a database.

Tacit knowledge is highly personal, difficult to express and transmit systematically. The barrier between explicit and tacit is not always crisp and can be porous, but the definitions are useful in the context of the legal sector.

Managing explicit knowledge

In the legal context how do you manage this explicit knowledge?

It is a mistake to try to codify and make available through information technology (IT) systems everything that lawyers 'know'. As Dave Snowden would say, we know more than we can say and we can say more than we can write down. The cost of trying to retrieve all a lawyer 'knows' would be immense and the return low, as even if it could be codified and kept updated, their co-workers wouldn't want to retrieve deep knowledge from a database, but would prefer to exchange knowledge through conversation.

There are, however, many aspects of lawyers' work that can usefully be codified for future use. The aim of codification is to make knowledge accessible to those who need it at the time that they need it. There is some cost in this: cost of man-hours and hardware, the cost of writing down that knowledge, of storage, updating and destruction. However, the cost of easily codified knowledge is usually repaid by increased leverage, increased client satisfaction with lower costs and increased profit in fixed or value-based billing.

Although many lawyers may feel that the majority of their work is too bespoke to be codified, lawyers are used to using precedents, which are an age-old form of codified explicit knowledge. Once they understand that codification is simply an extended version of a precedents database, they are often more receptive to the idea.

How do you develop codified knowledge?

There are three main steps:

1. Decide upon what knowledge is to be codified, what knowledge is suitable for codification and what knowledge is strategically important enough to codify.
2. Decide how best to deliver the knowledge to the end user.
3. Decide upon the best delivery method within the budget of the firm.

What knowledge within the firm is suitable for codification?

To decide whether knowledge will be suitable for codification within a knowledge management (KM) system (whether an online system or a simple paper system), the following questions could be considered:

- Can this information/knowledge be explained and written down fairly easily?
- Once written down, is this information/knowledge easy to understand by all levels of fee earner?
- How often is this knowledge/information needed?

- How often does this knowledge/information change?
- How many fee earners need this knowledge/information and where do they work?
- Who do the users trust? How do they evaluate knowledge/information for their use?
- How profitable/crucial to the business is the area of law this information/knowledge relates to?

A knowledge map may help (see Annex 5A).

The next step is to decide what knowledge is strategically important enough to be codified. Ask yourself what business goals codification would fulfil? If you are unsure, this job would suit a director of knowledge management or senior, KM literate partner, obviously with input from each team, as the individuals delivering the service will have the best idea about what can be usefully codified.

BOX 5.1   Knowledge in a legal firm suitable for codification

Some examples are:

- Forms
- Precedents
- Models to develop documents/improve drafting
- Practice notes
- Contact information – experts in litigation, external advisers, counsel
- Contact information for internal experts – people to pass clients to when cross-selling or people to discuss tricky problems with
- Commonly referred to background information – i.e. in clinical negligence cases this may be basic medical information about diseases or common operations, in a professional negligence case this may be checklists used by surveyors
- Checklists
- Workflows
- Client-based specific clauses/precedents (for larger/more frequent clients)
- Common clauses in tenders and supporting documentation
- Lists of current charge out rates
- Reading lists for lawyers and sources of additional information
- Lawyers' CVs and profiles, written for different audiences (tenders, authors' profiles, website information)

Codification may save money in the longer term, but will cost money in the short term. It is necessary therefore to do a cost-benefit analysis. Concentrate on developing those aspects which are strategically important for the business. What aspects are key business drivers? Which areas are showing good profits, good growth and have a positive future? Are there areas where there is repeat profitable activity? Are there different areas of the business performing the same process, even if the law is different (litigation is a common example)? Which clients are demanding more for less, but have potential to offer good cash-flow and plenty of on-going work? Is there an area where you have high staff turnover, high leverage or questionable quality, especially repeated mistakes? Do you have a team performing well in comparison to others who do similar work?

It is necessary to understand what the business drivers of your business are, and then focus on areas where codified knowledge will add value to the work that is done.

How to deliver the knowledge?

This next step may seem like jumping to the end of the process, but consider how the knowledge will be delivered, as this will have a distinct effect on how it ought to be stored.

Consider the following:

- Where will the knowledge be accessed? Will it be from various offices, a single office or from home?
- How often will it be used? Frequently or rarely?
- How often will the knowledge change?
- Who will be:
    - the users of this knowledge and what are their expectations in terms of performance, quality and availability?
    - the owners of the knowledge and how will quality be monitored?
    - responsible for maintenance and how often will there be updating? This is very different in different areas of law. How expensive will maintenance be?
    - the providers of knowledge and how and in what format will it be supplied and will this need conversion to suit the users?

Knowledge which needs to be accessed at a variety of fee earners' desks across the country, which is accessed frequently and changes regularly, will require a different solution to knowledge which rarely changes and needs to be accessed by a small number of fee earners in a single office.

Lastly, and obviously, cost considerations are a major part of this decision-making process and you will need to be clear about what funds are available over what timescale.

Online systems such as searchable document management systems of various guises, intranets, precedent databases, all have the following benefits:

- they are usually a single, structured point of contact for a range of knowledge needs;
- they are easily accessed across multiple offices;

- they can be accessible from out of the office;
- the cost of storage is low compared to print for most mid-sized firms' needs;
- changes can be made quickly and disseminated immediately.

However, they also have the following disadvantages:

- the cost of such systems is variable: a high cost for a bespoke system tailor-made by external consultants, a lower cost for adapting existing software for a new purpose;
- they will need specialist information technology (IT) support, although this can be purchased as required and needn't involve a full-time IT department;
- users will need training;
- users will require a period of time to bring themselves up to speed on the system and will work more slowly for that period;
- systems have to be designed around users needs, or the system will not be used;
- the system will need regular updating (new knowledge added, old knowledge removed) to maintain trust in it;
- without a clear policy for destroying old knowledge, they can easily become overwhelming.

If you think you have found an online system that is appropriate for your firm's needs, speak to your IT department or those that deal with IT for you if you have outsourced it. No particular systems are recommended here because they become obsolete very quickly, but your IT contacts will know what is currently available and also perhaps what will be most cost-effective.

Paper-based systems can still be useful and shouldn't be ignored. They have the following benefits:

- they are simple to set up and use;
- they require little or no training for fee earners.

However, there are disadvantages:

- they are geographically limited (multiple identical systems are not a good idea);
- they cannot be used on multiple sites, by multiple users simultaneously;
- they can be more difficult to keep up to date.

When deciding what to include in your system and how to deliver it, you may find it helpful to use Kano Model analysis, developed by Dr Noriaki Kano in the 1980s.[1] This model is more usually used for developing products such as mobile telephones for sale to customers, but is similarly useful in designing services for internal clients. Its simplicity is one of its strengths.

Simply ask your internal clients (the fee earners who will be using the database/KM system) to grade attributes as:

1. threshold (necessary for them to use the system);
2. performance (not necessary, but improve enjoyment and usability of the system);
3. excitement (clients don't know that they want, but these improve enjoyment of the service); or
4. not relevant.

Cut out all the irrelevant aspects of service, include all the threshold aspects and include performance and excitement as your budget allows. Don't forget to budget for ongoing costs, which includes the manpower necessary to keep whatever system you choose up to date in the future. Whilst using a legally trained member of staff for this may seem costly, they will have valuable experience of working as a lawyer which forms a cultural back-drop to their discussions. The discussions are likely to be shorter (cultural understanding) and better (fewer misunderstandings) which can mean the project overall is cheaper to implement.

Aim for usability, relevance and usefulness.

Measure the value of the system and keep those measurements under review (see Chapter 9 for more detailed information about measurement). Don't rely on an existing managing partner's enthusiasm. Have figures or anecdotes to explain the successes and failures.

If you are creating an intranet for your business, you will probably need to organise your content under a taxonomy so that it can easily be found at a later date.[2] Alternatively you could use a 'folksonomy', where your users tag content with key words; although few law firms find that a pure folksonomy works for them, most have at least a basic framework taxonomy supplemented by a folksonomy.

Avoiding common pitfalls

The primary common pitfall has already been discussed. This is trying to codify all knowledge instead of discriminating and only codifying that knowledge which is readily codifiable. Stick to precedents, workflows/checklists/case management systems, practice notes and/or commonly needed background information.

The second most common pitfall in codification and managing explicit knowledge is an excessive focus on technology and the delegation of development of the system to the IT department or external IT specialists, liaising with junior members of staff. Whilst an IT-based solution may be sensible, it has to work in a way that the end users need it to, otherwise it will not succeed. Although it may seem expensive to take experienced lawyers away from fee earning to become involved in development, user testing and validation, this will be less costly overall than a bespoke IT system which no one uses. Davenport and Prusak suggest a 2/3:1/3 ratio in relation to KM projects.[3] The majority of the time, effort and money should be spent on non-IT factors such as content, organisational culture, motivation, etc. Only a third of the time, effort and budget should be on IT. If you find that your project is straying too far from this ratio, you should step back from the project and reassess it.

Another common pitfall is to assume either that the firm's work is too bespoke for an outsourced provider to adequately satisfy the firm's needs or that the external provider's precedents will necessarily be better than in-house ones. Investigate outsourced systems for cost and value. When balancing the cost of internally developed and externally provided precedents, don't forget to take into account the ongoing cost of maintenance. Some areas of law move slowly and precedents stay valid for years; other areas are fast moving and use of an old precedent may cause professional negligence issues. Whether an internally developed precedent bank will be less expensive than a PLC/LNB one, will depend on the field of law, the type of work undertaken, the clients involved and the firm's branding. Trust in the knowledge is paramount. Personally, I have lost count of the number of times that I have heard fee earners say 'We have XYZ on our intranet but I don't use it because I'm not sure who wrote it and I'm not sure if it is up to date.' If the end users don't trust the content of the knowledge system, it will be a waste of money.

To make a new database project work, you will need to invest time in it, not just time to develop and implement the project, but time to train the staff and time for the staff to get used to the new system. Many systems fail because all the investment is in development rather than training. To suit different learners and different fee earners and to keep everyone on board, the training will need to be offered in a variety of ways: a combination of classroom-based learning, walk-the-floor question answering and one-to-one desk-based learning.

Lastly, other common pitfalls are failing to address the needs of all types of stakeholders to get KM champions on board and address the needs of snipers, and failing to ensure that there are some members of staff who are formally responsible for KM. Whilst not all firms can afford to have a dedicated Head of KM and numerous professional support lawyers (PSLs), those who want to have successful knowledge projects will need staff whose roles include this responsibility alongside their other work. There are certain skills that a knowledge worker needs, not to mention being informed about much of the theory and practice surrounding KM, which every fee earner cannot have.

Improving a firm's knowledge-sharing culture

This section applies to explicit and tacit knowledge equally, but has been placed in this chapter as it often crops up as a key issue in a firm new to KM which is trying to get contributions for a new precedent or knowledge database.

Culture is inherently stable. You may be able to change how workers work, bringing in an IT system or changing reporting lines, but it is extremely difficult to change employees' minds about what is the appropriate way to deal with each other, how to approach difficult problems or how they value team work.

How can you understand your firm's culture? Ed Schein's theory is a good place to start. According to him, in his book *Organizational Culture and Leadership*,[4] there are three layers to understanding a business's culture: artefacts, espoused values and basic assumptions. Have a look at your firm's artefacts: are you an open plan, all inclusive, kind of firm? Have a look at the espoused values: what is your business's vision statement if you have such a thing? If not, what does your organisation plan look like and what do you say in your advertising, in your brochure and on your website? What are your business's basic assumptions: who did you promote, employ or reject last year and why?

While there is little point in confronting the whole of an organisation's culture head on and trying to change it, there is no reason why you can't chip away at the negative aspects that prevent good knowledge sharing and try to improve what you have. You will just need to be realistic about what is achievable and not get disheartened when changes seem to take a long time. If you have a significant change to make, you might want to read a little further into change management theory and divide the project into future, current and transition states. Then designate some change agents and sponsors, even though most firms will simply need some steering, rather than a wholesale change of direction.

The key to a good knowledge sharing culture is trust. Users need to trust the quality of the content they are being asked to use. Providers need to trust that their contributions are being used appropriately by the right people and that giving away their knowledge won't negatively affect their power base within their firm. If maintainers have responsibility for keeping knowledge updated, they need to know that senior staff value the time they spend on this.

Without trust the most sophisticated system will eventually fail. That trust must be visible, not just declared to be important. Staff must see that knowledge-sharing is recognised and rewarded in a way that is meaningful to them.

Face-to-face contact is an important part of creating trust. Many people would rather talk to a semi-specialist that they know and trust than a purported expert that they do not know. You do not need to schedule a lot of expensive meetings to build rapport; simply remember to consider including face-to-face meetings where appropriate in training and business development meetings and/or video conferencing.

Most firms would like to get to the point when knowledge-sharing is 'simply how we do things', but this positive culture takes a while to become ingrained and requires effort on multiple fronts. There is no simple answer to getting this right and one of the first places to begin is in recruitment. Don't just hire bright lawyers; look for those who are also intellectually curious and whose natural tendency is to discuss their work and mentor others.

Once you gradually have the right staff coming into your firm, support their knowledge-sharing efforts with the right rewards and recognition. Here, it is important that KM strategy is aligned to human resources strategy and firm culture. It won't matter how much the firm talks about how important the KM strategy is to the firm if it rewards those who bill high and share nothing. This is the clearest signal of what is valued by the firm. Having knowledge work considered in appraisals and knowledge targets set for individuals is an excellent message for senior staff to send, but if their actions do not support the message, it will have little positive effect.[5] Once one gets beyond promotions, bonuses and salary, rewards for knowledge-sharing can be more prone to 'gaming' whereby staff consciously or unconsciously give more of whatever is being measured to get the reward. If you simply measure number of contributions to a KM database you may receive many poor quality contributions, rather than the quality contributions you need. One reward system that many other industries use is to reward knowledge-sharing with knowledge-related rewards, so an individual who has made a certain number of valuable contributions to a knowledge database is given a ticket to a conference they wish to attend or a training course they are particularly interested in. This hopefully sets up a virtuous circle of knowledge-sharing and knowledge-development.

Many Heads of KM report that acts of recognition are excellent for improving knowledge-sharing. These could be any means of recognising someone's efforts and thanking them for that effort: personal thanks, public thanks, tokens such as chocolate coins. It is important to note that it is the recognition which is the important aspect, not the token itself. Also, when times are difficult, one has to be sensitive to a fee earner not wanting to appear to have too little fee earning work to do, so sometimes private thanks may be more appropriate and appreciated than public thanks.

Top-down support for a knowledge-sharing culture is important, although if you don't have it, there is still much that can be done from the bottom up, by focusing initially on key stakeholders and new starters. With this strategy it is important to build wide support, so that your plan can survive changes of personnel. Informing staff about the benefits of KM can be a big part of changing minds and all new starters and trainees ought to be given training not only in how to use the KM systems, but in the expectations that the firm has of them to share what they know and what precedents and documents they develop. There are further thoughts about how to inform staff about the benefits of KM in Annex 5C: Building a KM buzz.

Some of the common pitfalls to avoid in creating your knowledge-sharing culture are:

- Derogation of all derivative ideas or non-home-grown ideas – sometimes the best ideas are built on already existing knowledge.
- Anti-bragging culture – this culture has other benefits, but can inhibit knowledge-sharing as staff deny they are doing anything unusually good and do not offer to help others.
- A tough, eat-what-you-kill culture – if it is seen as weakness to ask another for the benefit of their expertise, knowledge will not be shared.
- Fear of redundancies – knowledge is undoubtedly power and those who fear they will soon need to look elsewhere for work will want to sell their unique knowledge to a new employer. Sometimes you cannot prevent the redundancies, but firms must take this loss into account when contemplating them.
- Failure to walk-the-walk as well as talk-the-talk – if hoarders thrive in a firm it won't matter what are declared as the firm's KM objectives.
- Trying to break all silos[6] – whilst everyone would prefer that silos didn't exist, concentrate your efforts on those silos that are having a negative effect on your business. If you have silos that are working quite well alone and not negatively affecting the firm, consider them to be a low priority.

Summary – the least you need to know:

- Codification is best suited to explicit knowledge, including:

  - workflows and case management;
  - precedents;
  - knowledge databases;
  - intranets.

- A firm's knowledge-sharing culture will take years to develop, but can be supported by:
  - hiring the right staff;
  - senior support;
  - bottom-up training and support;
  - the right reward structure and tokens of recognition;
  - fostering trust – in the quality of the knowledge and the value placed upon it.

ANNEX 5A: Assembling a knowledge map

I first came across the idea of 'knowledge maps' reading Davenport and Prusak's *Working Knowledge*. I was struck immediately by how sensible the idea seemed, particularly for a sector such as the legal sector where so much of the knowledge that I wanted to 'manage' was a combination of explicit codifiable knowledge and difficult to codify tacit knowledge, and it was difficult to engage fee earners with IT solutions.

A knowledge map is a map of where a person may find the knowledge that they seek. It could be a knowledge 'White Pages' or a cleverly constructed database or even a real map. It doesn't contain the knowledge itself, but points the seeker in the right direction: it is a navigation aid. It has some overlap with organisation charts or office directories, but focuses on knowledge. It can also work as an inventory, highlighting gaps in knowledge which the business can work to fill.

A knowledge map covers explicit and tacit knowledge and enables an organisation to understand its strengths and weaknesses, which can inform KM strategies and choice of applications.

What kind of knowledge map will work for your firm?

Most of the information that you would need to include in the knowledge map is probably already within your firm, but is fragmented or within the knowledge of your staff. You will need to talk to staff and follow trails of recommendations to develop a formal map which is searchable by topic or key words.

The key factors in a successful knowledge map, whether paper or online, are ease of use, clarity, searchability and accuracy.

A paper-based map such as a file of entries, a card-file or a rolodex, has the benefit of being low cost, save for the time spent in setting it up. Unfortunately, unless your staff turnover is low and your staff very senior and knowledgeable at the outset, this will quickly become out of date as people leave and join and develop additional areas of expertise. Trust, which is an extremely important aspect of any knowledge management system, will quickly be lost in the map. It will also be difficult to share the map widely, especially if you have more than one office.

An online solution will be easier to update and distribute. The costs of set up may be greater, but there is no reason why this can't be a dual purpose system, combining standard CVs or profiles for use in tenders, contact details for the firm's telephone directory as well as knowledge specialisms. An online solution can also include not just a photo, but perhaps also a short video clip from the individual explaining their areas of interest and expertise.

Knowledge maps, like organisation charts, are political documents and depending upon the culture at a firm, one can end up with too few people admitting to expertise because of fear of censure for bragging, inability to appreciate their level of expertise or perceived additional non-chargeable work which will follow, or people can inappropriately claim expertise and exert pressure to be well situated compared to others. It is because knowledge is a valuable asset that this isn't straightforward, so in some ways it is a good sign if this is difficult to manage in your firm: it shows how highly people's expertise is valued. To solve these problems, look at peer review and nomination rather than asking each individual to nominate their own specialism and administer their own entries.[7]

Digressing slightly, when I practised as a fee earner within law firms, I noticed how it wasn't always my supervisor, a senior partner, who I wanted to discuss issues with. In fact, one lunchtime, my colleagues and I devised an alternative supervision scheme whereby instead of the traditional static model of one partner supervising three junior fee earner for all aspects of their work, different experienced fee earners (whatever their notional rank) were designated as specialists in certain fields. The idea was that when one had a query about civil procedure one visited the civil procedure Tsar, or when one wondered whether or how to negotiate a settlement one approached the case strategy Tsar, etc. Although a knowledge map doesn't necessitate a change to the traditional model of supervision, it allows fee earners to identify and access the right expert for the right question, maximising the quality of advice.

Social network analysis

If yours is a larger firm or you have the resources, Social Network Analysis (SNA) is a useful tool alongside a knowledge map. SNA maps and measures the relationships between staff, groups, organisations and computers and shows the flows between them. SNA can show who is closely connected within a firm, who is a contributor to knowledge flows and who is on the periphery. Peripheral individuals are often sources of untapped knowledge and well-connected individuals are not always the most senior, yet can be a significant loss to a firm if they leave. SNA allows firms to understand and work with its existing networks, managing them more effectively, support less cohesive groups and anticipate potential problems. There is some suggested further reading about SNA in Appendix 2.

ANNEX 5B: Case study – Burges Salmon's KM system

Burges Salmon's view-point

Who is Burges Salmon?

Burges Salmon is a leading UK law firm working across the full breadth of major practice areas. Their clients range from listed companies, private individuals and central government to charities and private businesses. They are known for their open and collaborative culture.

The challenge

Burges Salmon has always invested in a wide range of high quality internal and external legal information and knowledge resources. However, these resources were available to lawyers on disparate applications or were developed piecemeal, so there was little consistent functionality. Search capability was variable between applications and not as effective as it could have been and there was a business need to simplify and improve the existing systems.

Initial user feedback on existing systems asked for a means to search internal and external resources simultaneously in a simple 'Google-style' front end.

The system would need to search around 1.5 million documents, preserve document security and fully integrate with the document management system as well as other internal applications.

The selection process

Burges Salmon undertook a competitive tender process including local and national knowledge management system providers. The project team developed an unbiased scorecard system to assess the responses against set criteria. GateWest's 'University-in-a-box' (UIB), a non-legal sector product which uses Autonomy's enterprise search software, consistently came out top in all areas, including functionality, flexibility and added value.

GateWest provided a Proof of Concept of the UIB tool and continuous feedback from key stakeholders and trial groups was used to refine the product to suit the legal sector and Burges Salmon in particular.

The solution

University-in-a-box is GateWest New Media's knowledge and learning portal powered by Autonomy's Intelligent Data Operating Lawyer (IDOL) technology. Autonomy's IDOL infrastructure layer allows computers to form a conceptual and contextual understanding of any piece of electronic data, including unstructured information (text, email, voice or video). It enables a single interface for users to search across Interwoven (which combines document management, email management and mobility access) and our previous SQL databases (which held precedents and know-how across the firm).

The Burges Salmon system has nine different department/unit knowledge zones. Each department home page contains different collections of key documents, news channels, announcements, website hotlinks and a link to the concept search element of the UIB tool. There is an easy link to an automatic submission form for the firm's know-how system and access to the legacy know-how and precedent taxonomies.

Success factors

Burges Salmon felt that the key success factors were:

- Close co-operation between PSLs, knowledge management partners and trial groups, helped to keep stakeholders engaged and interested and provided continuous feedback to refine the solution.
- Training in the new system was by tailored training sessions and floor walking by the KM team.
- The expertise of the IT department on knowledge management systems and legal knowledge issues.

Results

Although it was originally anticipated that the system would search across 1.5 million documents, after iManage documents were included at the request of lawyers in fast moving areas, the system now searches around 15 million documents.

There has been overwhelmingly positive feedback from lawyers about the system, highlighting the time saved and how they can now find materials they didn't even know the firm had:

'More in hope than expectation I typed in 'Presumption against retrospective legisla-tion'. The second most relevant documentation contained just what I wanted.'

' ... it certainly makes any other knowledge management systems I have used seem antiquated!'

'The KMS is far superior to an iManage or PLC search and astonishing results can be found.'

'It is possible to find buried references in documents on the KMS which conven-tional searching would not turn up.'

GateWest's view-point

GateWest have a long history of developing knowledge management and e-learning systems for demanding customers such as BAE Systems and ABN Amro Bank, and were excited by the opportunity to bid for the KM project at Burges Salmon. This enthusiasm was fuelled by the realisation that Burges Salmon clearly understood the value of their collective knowledge, and that the only 'product' that a law firm has to sell is that accumulated expertise and experience. That Burges Salmon shared the same vision as GateWest for KM gave the company the confidence to invest in the sales campaign.

The sales campaign itself was both a steep learning curve and a more protracted process than was anticipated. The first hurdle to overcome was purely cultural, and it was soon evident that the language of law firms is unique to them. There are no 'customers', only 'clients'. There are no 'projects' or 'orders', only 'matters', which the client has 'instructed' the 'firm' to act on his/her behalf. Next step in understanding the law firm environment in general and Burges Salmon in particular was the recognition of the document management system (DMS), iManage, as the foundation and source of the internally generated expertise, and its place in the technical landscape required to achieve the vision.

Following the initial invitation to tender, which eliminated all but two suppliers, GateWest were delighted to be invited to a 'proof of concept' phase, often called a 'bake-off', where a comparison could be made between the solution proposed and the offering from what is the market leader in supplying US and UK law firms with KM systems. Over a three-month period Burges Salmon refined what they believed to be the optimum solution, inviting both competitors to demonstrate how their system could be tailored to meet the firm's requirements. Due to a combination of technical flexibility, a willingness to customise software, and a team orientated approach GateWest were delighted to be awarded the contract.

GateWest are very pleased that the project has been received so well by the most important people in this exercise, the end users of the system, those 'knowledge workers'. The reasons for the success of the project seem simple but then simple does not mean easy!

What GateWest believe has led to the enthusiastic reaction to the system is a result of:

- A world class technology platform of Autonomy IDOL, iManage and GateWest's UIB.
- A common vision between GateWest and Burges Salmon of the KM system and what it will deliver.
- GateWest's willingness to adapt its core product and create new software function-ality.
- The teamwork between the technical staff in both organisations.

And finally:

- The relentless energy, enthusiasm and evangelical zeal of the business team involved in specifying, deploying and training. Awesome!

ANNEX 5C: Building a KM buzz

Unless a firm understands the value of KM within its business and the contribution it currently makes and potentially could make to efficiency and profitability, it will not invest adequately in it. Even if a knowledge department has survived recent cuts, it will not receive an adequate share of future increased budgets unless key decision-makers within the firm appreciate the benefits this would bring. Marketing KM internally within your firm cannot be an 'added extra'. A campaign to market KM internally can improve usage of existing systems, improve collaboration and build a better knowledge-sharing culture, key goals of all KM professionals. You would not expect a law firm to simply rely on its reputation for excellent legal work without marketing itself; similarly you should not fail to market your KM work internally.

Of course most law firms have marketing budgets and most knowledge departments do not; however, it is possible to create a successful buzz about your KM work on a budget and the following four simple ideas are a recommended starting point:

1. Persuade a sceptic

You cannot market KM alone. You will need a network of champions to spread the word and build the right culture. You probably already know key figures within the firm who 'get' KM and before now have probably concentrated your efforts on them, but try to persuade a few sceptics as well. Just as reformed smokers often turn into the most zealous anti-smokers, reformed KM-sceptics can become your greatest champions. Start by discovering some of the challenges and bugbears of your notable KM-sceptics and see if you can help them. One-to-one meetings are usually the best way to gather this kind of information, rather than team meetings, emails or surveys. Lawyers can be surprisingly anxious about peer approval and so they need to feel safe in admitting to their difficulties and not risk losing face.

If you can help a sceptic with one of their key difficulties or make their life easier, you will hopefully convert them and gain a vocal champion. If you can demonstrably improve their profitability as well, by reducing write-offs or improving chargeable time or billing, you will also have some clear evidence of a KM success to persuade other sceptics.

2. A campaign to pick some low-hanging fruit

Investigate some of the smaller, simpler problems that fee earners experience, ones that you suspect your existing KM systems can already help with. Choose those which will be the easiest to solve and plan a campaign of fixing a number of those problems during a short period of time. The key to this tactic is to solve a large number of smaller problems in order to create some water-cooler chat about how helpful you, your staff and your KM systems are.

3. Leverage your existing solutions

No doubt you already have some well-thought through solutions to common issues, but do all your fee earners understand everything that you offer or how your systems can make their lives easier, improve their figures and minimise their most boring tasks? You probably trained them all in using your systems once, but think about all the fantastic things your word-processing package can do and how many of the facilities you actually use. You probably had some training when you first started using the package, but how much of it do you remember on an ongoing basis? It is probably the same for your fee earners using your intranet/knowledge-store/precedent database. Plan some additional training, preferably desk-based one-to-ones, and create a buzz about the scope of your systems without spending additional money on new IT.

4. Market yourself

Lastly, ensure that everyone hears about your successes. Your firm's marketing team can probably spare a little time to pass on to you some of the skills needed to create your KM buzz, although most KM professionals are already expert in client-facing KM marketing work and so probably know more than they think.

Why not try some of the following:

- A monthly/quarterly lunchtime meeting to explain what is happening within KM in your firm, or a networking mixer-event.
- A regular e-newsletter highlighting your current KM activity.
- A regular KM impact report for the Executive Board, providing a brief summary of the benefits of KM in terms of economic and social results.
- Submit KM success stories for inclusion in any existing internal marketing.
- Have a 'big theme' workshop (internal or for clients) on KM.

Lastly, remember that if you increase take-up of your existing KM solutions, you will be improving the efficiency and profitability of your firm, so creating a KM buzz is in your firm's best interests.

Endnotes

1. Read more about Kano model analysis at **www.mindtools.com/pages/article/ newCT_97.htm** (accessed 10 April 2012).
2. There is an excellent practical description of how to create a taxonomy, either using a software programme or manually in Rumizen, M. (2002) *The Complete Idiot's Guide to Knowledge Management*, CWL Publishing Enterprises, chapter 14.
3. Davenport, T. and Prusak, L. (2000) *Working Knowledge* Harvard Business School Press, p. 173.
4. Schein, E. (1997) *Organizational Culture and Leadership*, Jossey-Bass.
5. Chapter 8, Annex 8C includes a discussion with Mark Gould about rewards and recognition.
6. Silos are groups where people rarely share knowledge outside their group and usually do not take non-group members into account when making decisions.

7   There are more ideas of how to gather the right information for knowledge maps and expert databases in Chapter 6.

Chapter 6

Managing tacit knowledge

This chapter will familiarise you with the following:

- What 'tacit knowledge' is and what 'knowledge' and 'wisdom' are
- How to 'manage' tacit knowledge
- The what, when and how of storytelling
- The what, when and how of after action learning
- The importance of know-who as well as know-how
- How to retain knowledge within your firm when your staff leave

---

What is 'tacit knowledge' and how do you manage it?

It is probably easier to start by saying what tacit knowledge isn't. It isn't anything easily codified. It isn't formulae, maps, objective instructions and things that can be easily put into words. It isn't the court rules or the Companies Act.

Tacit knowledge is your understanding of things. It is judgement and insights. It is subjective; it is experience; it is 'canniness' or 'nous'. It is that special gut feeling you get after years of practice, knowing when to fight a case to trial and when to settle. It is hard to express, let alone transmit or codify in any logical manner into a database. And it is extremely valuable.[1]

There has historically been a massive debate about whether knowledge and in particular tacit knowledge can be managed at all. Knowledge after all resides in people's heads.

Whereas explicit knowledge can be codified in a straightforward manner and placed in a database for all to access, it is doubtful whether much of people's tacit knowledge can be codified in this way.

The best way to leverage tacit knowledge is to concentrate on connecting people, developing networks, communities of practice and white pages. Technology may be useful, although much is lost when interactions aren't face to face and when you are dealing in knowledge that is not easy to express, that lost aspect is likely to be the most important aspect. Technologies which connect people, making it easier to find the right person to then start a conversation, or to connect people remotely, are the most useful. Because this kind of knowledge transfer is so dependent on connecting people, it will be greatly affected by who works at your firm and your firm's culture. For this reason, read the suggestions for different ways of connecting people and take a few that suit your firm. You may even find that some suit one team and others suit different groups. I recommend that you simply work with these differences rather than trying to force everyone to work to a standard practice. Have a few pilot schemes and stick with the methods that work for you and drop those that don't.

Why should you care about tacit knowledge?

In this information age, a vast amount of information is available online. One of your clients may at this very moment be trying to look up the answer to their boundary dispute on the web. Many Acts of Parliament are online and there are no doubt many willing paralegals with a smattering of knowledge and narrow experience willing to tell them what the law is. What a good law firm has to sell, which your clients can't find on the web, is its combined tacit knowledge, its combined years of experience of dealing with similar cases – knowing the local courts, knowing the best tactics to move a dispute towards settlement, when to mediate, when to threaten court. This tacit knowledge is a law firm's unique selling point (USP).

Larger manufacturing businesses recognise the importance of the tacit knowledge gained through working alongside others in different jobs and commonly transfer managers though different departments to ensure that they gain experience and knowledge before taking senior roles. Although there is a cost in their learning curve, their development means their later decisions are more informed and so of better quality.

The sharing of tacit knowledge can be supported by connecting people to share conversations, including:

- Face-to-face solutions:
    - mentoring and supervision;
    - knowledge fairs;
    - storytelling;
    - after action learning;
    - Gurteen knowledge cafes;
    - 'ask an expert' coffee mornings and talk rooms.

- Online solutions:
    - supporting communities of practice;
    - collaborative ICT tools, synchronous and asynchronous;
    - White Pages, expert directories.

Why/how does 'connecting people' work so well?

Conversation, according to Alan Webber,[2] is the most important form of work. Conversation is the way that those who work in knowledge-intense fields such as law, share what they know with others in the firm, discover what they know and what they don't yet know, and who knows what. It may be an informal method of knowledge-sharing, which is somewhat hit and miss, but it is a powerful tool and one which also has the benefit of serendipity. Different disciplines look at problems in different ways and unusual pairings in conversations often generate new and unusual solutions and ideas. Conversation has always been somewhat stifled at law firms because of the focus on chargeable time, but recent moves towards working from home have hit this form of knowledge sharing in all industries.

People with similar training understand the context of each other's questions better than people of different training. If an experienced lawyer asked another experienced lawyer in the same field for the solution to a query, the resulting solution would be very different in content and timeframe to the solution you would get if you asked a lawyer from a different field of expertise. The solution and timeframe would be different again if you asked a law librarian or a law student. And you would get a different solution again if you asked all three to collaborate on a joint solution, each bringing their particular skills to the task. You get better results by bringing the right people closer to each other, although unusual pairings can spark different avenues of investigation and make both parties question their assumptions about what their solution ought to look like. And people understand the context of the question far better than any search engine or hierarchical taxonomy.

Many Japanese businesses have set up 'talk rooms'[3] to connect staff and encourage this less-predictable creative blending and exchange. Researchers are expected to visit the talk room for 20 to 30 minutes a day and drink green tea and converse with their colleagues about their work. This format might not easily translate into UK law firms, but a similar purpose could be fulfilled in a formal way by creating 'ask an expert' coffee mornings[4] or lunches or informally by encouraging staff to mix before and after training sessions or business development meetings.

Face-to-face meetings are ideal. You know yourself that you trust information that you get from people you have met and had the opportunity to size up yourself, far more than an unknown person touted as an expert. When you size people up, you are using a complex variety of skills to ascertain your views on the quality of what they say, much of which you aren't aware of using.

The important aspect for those trying to encourage this kind of knowledge exchange is that a firm should invest in the facilitation of the conversation, not in trying to capture and codify the content.

Preventing loss of knowledge

One of the major problems with tacit knowledge is that it tends to be lost once your fee earners leave your firm. You can keep any documents which have codified their explicit knowledge, but you lose their experience and insight.

Most firms have experienced the disruption that this causes. Sometimes it is the retirement of a long-standing, knowledgeable expert in a particular field, whose retirement begins the slow loss of clients, who realise that no one who remains in the firm quite understands their needs as the retiree did. Sometimes it is the loss of a long-standing member of the administration team, who was on first name terms with many key clients and who knew how to get the best out of a creaky old IT system.

The Tennessee Valley Authority, the world's biggest producer of electric power, concerned about the looming problem of retiring baby boomers, decided to tackle the problem of loss of knowledge through staff attrition in 1999.[5] They created a People Team who divided the problem into a three part process: What, So What, and Now What?

They began by looking at who was retiring when, then identified those people whose knowledge would be most missed by the business when they left. They did this by interviewing staff and asking them when they would like to retire and what they worried would be lost when they left. Once they had lists of potential knowledge losses (the What), they analysed their importance (the So What), as obviously some losses would have long-term effects and others could be recreated and relearned or would be superseded by new knowledge. Once the areas of knowledge loss were prioritised, they looked at potential solutions (the Now What), which included codifying the knowledge where possible, training by existing staff or eliminating the need for that knowledge.

Of course your business is very unlikely to need such a large scale systematic approach to staff attrition, but you will need to keep a note of who is likely to leave and when, and make sure that their loss won't be devastating for your business, and you can use the What, So What and Now What framework to prepare for their departure.

You can capture and codify to some extent people's experiences once you know that they are leaving by video-taping their experiences and/or creating a book of their successful case studies/lessons learned, or by having them work side-by-side with their replacement for a short while, but this relies on their being cooperative, which may be true for a partner choosing to retire, but is less true of an ambitious junior lawyer leaving for a rival firm or someone being made redundant. In this case there is not much you can do if you have not made any efforts at knowledge sharing during their employment with you.

Prevention is of course better than cure, so the rest of the chapter focuses on ways to connect staff in order to transfer knowledge between fee earners so that hopefully when one leaves, much of their useful knowledge has already been transferred to the remaining staff.

One-to-one knowledge sharing

Mentoring and supervision

Supervision is very common in law firms. All fee earners expect to be supervised and audited to some extent. The extent of supervision may vary depending on experience, but it is the natural way that lawyers and law firms manage the risk of negligence claims and share their experiences. If you review the knowledge spiral discussed in Chapter 2 (see Figure 2.3), you will see how supervision fits well within the socialisation quadrant, the top left-hand one, which showed how tacit knowledge is passed on.

Mentoring is less common in law firms, but it is an excellent way for staff to share tacit knowledge as it includes all the knowledge-sharing of supervision without any fear on the part of the junior lawyer of admitting inadequacies in their knowledge. A mentoring system is quite easy to set up within a firm. After some training, most professionals could offer mentoring to more junior members of staff and a firm could make it an expectation that each fee earner mentors someone more junior, perhaps people three years' Post Qualification Experience (PQE) below them, and be responsible for their learning and development.

The difficulties can be in the relationships and in the levels of expertise that each party has. The lawyer you want to supervise you on client relationship issues may be very different to the lawyer you want to advise you on the law of boundary disputes.

One-to-many and many-to-many knowledge sharing

Collaborative work tools

Just because knowledge is tacit, doesn't mean that it is impossible to make it explicit. Storytelling (see Box 6.1 below) is a strong medium to pass on the nuggets of knowledge held tacitly. It may sound a bit 'new-agey', but these could be stories about client care situations handled well or badly, stories about managing networks and networking skills, introductions and conversations, which can all be held within a database or ICT solution. Blogs and discussion boards are also an excellent ICT solution to the need to codify tacit knowledge.

Collaborative ICT tools

Collaborative tools, usually offered via a firm's intranet, can be of two main types: synchronous and asynchronous. Synchronous tools are those which promote remote sharing and person-to-person contact over the electronic media. They include presentation tools, video conferencing, chat, voting, video and audio systems. Asynchronous tools are those which allow others to deposit knowledge and thoughts onto the system at any time they choose and include discussion software and message boards. Both synchronous and asynchronous collaborative tools can facilitate conversation and support communities of practice (see below). People often refer to groupware such as SharePoint when discussing collaborative ICT tools, but there are many other systems which can be adapted to do the same. Talk to your IT experts to see what is available and what would suit your firm. A smaller firm could use Skype and desktops with web cams, instead of investing in expensive video conferencing facilities. Email can even be used to facilitate collaboration, although message/discussion boards have more options and are generally more easily searchable afterwards. Each firm will be slightly different and no collaborative tool is right in all situations. It is worth doing some investigating to get the right package of ICT for your firm.

A tool with information richness, such as video-conferencing for meetings, or videoed presentations, transmits more knowledge than documents alone, as the viewer picks up a surprising amount from facial expressions, tone, inflexion and body language.

To ensure that ICT collaborative tools are actually used by fee earners, you may need to consider policies and procedures for use and to work on a culture of openness, sharing and discussion. For the community to work there will need to be sufficient everyday-contributors and users, and sufficient expert-contributors, to build trust in the content.[6]

BOX 6.1 Storytelling

As previously discussed, storytelling is an excellent way to pass on experiences and tacit knowledge and has been used by many large organisations, including IBM and the World Bank. It is one of the few ways that different perspectives on topics can be brought out. Karl Weick says 'people think narratively rather than argumentatively or paradigmatically'.[7] Stories tend to be rich and complex and wholly suitable for elucidating the meaning in complex situations and events.

One of the important aspects to successful storytelling is for the event to be described in the voice of the person involved, as so much of what needs to be imparted is difficult to write down, but can be picked up by readers.

Although many lawyers may be somewhat sceptical of a technique which sounds so 'new-agey', most fee earners are natural storytellers. I often found when I was a junior lawyer in litigation that when I asked a more experienced

---

lawyer for the answer to a tricky technical issue, they would not usually simply tell me the answer, but more often would explain it within the context of a case they had been involved in which neatly illustrated the technical point. In that situation it was easier for them to explain complex ideas through narrative and easier for me, the listener, to retain the lesson that way. The common law develops through case law and it is the way that UK lawyers learn at university, so it is a very natural way for lawyers to share lessons in technical law. Similarly, trial lawyers will confirm the importance of developing a narrative that speaks to the facts in a civil or criminal trial to explain the claim or defence. It can be difficult in a civil claim to run a successful defence by simply putting a claimant to proof; usually the defence needs some form of narrative of an alternative explanation for the facts as well.

How can you use storytelling in law firms? When the then Department for Trade and Industry developed its storytelling database about developing White Papers for government, it arranged workshops at which discussion was based around memorable events along a timeline, noting positive and negative anecdotes, which were then anonymised into metaphorical tales. The resulting knowledge was turned into a map, stories and skills cards. The stories were interspersed with real-world examples of how the metaphorical stories applied. In the legal sector, if you wanted to put stories online, they could be linked to practice notes or precedents and one could overcome lawyers' dislike of the 'new agey' title by calling the resultant anecdotes 'war stories' or 'case studies'.

Communities of practice (COPs)

Communities of practice (COPs) are nothing new, but as knowledge has become more important within the business world, organisations have taken more notice of them.

Larger law firms, or those firms which are geographically diverse, will probably be more interested in COPs than smaller single office firms.

'Communities of practice' are groups of people who share a concern, an interest or a set of problems and interact with each other on an ongoing basis as a result. These people won't necessarily work together, but they will meet because they find value in their interactions. As they spend time together they typically share information, insight and advice. They help each other share problems, seeking to take advantage of their relationship.[8]

The things that differentiate communities of practice from departments or teams are the fuzzy boundaries, which often reach across formal groups and the goals of the COP. Whereas teams tend to be formed for specific purposes and work together to fulfil those goals, COPs may have stated goals, but these often fluctuate and each member may have different goals to other members. Teams and departments last as long as the business needs them, but COPs last as long as the members want them to last. Members of a COP are self-motivated to share knowledge and so are valuable to businesses.

For example, in a law firm, a COP could develop around a change in the law which affects multiple areas of specialism, such as a change to costs, or a

COP could develop around changes which affect particular clients who use multiple areas of law, such as when there are structural changes to NHS. The COPs in these situations could aim to help employees understand the changes better, sharing information about them and experiences in adapting to new ways of working and suggest common adaptations their precedents. As participants are self-motivated and supportive, knowledge-sharing is often of high quality.

How a business supports a community of practice will depend upon that business. COPs are easy to kill with too much top-down interference and difficult to create. The organic growth of COPs is a necessary part of their existence. That is not to say that a business cannot support COPs. Often, face-to-face networking is the best way to support COPs, through workshops and meetings, but ICT systems can facilitate COPs which reach across different geographical locations but have naturally strong trust in and understanding of each other.

Although COPs can be created from scratch for a particular purpose, most organisations find the most efficient thing to do is to support existing COPs which have developed by themselves, by providing adequate ICT such as through blogs, wikis and discussion boards[9] or networking support and perhaps also leadership from a champion/sponsor.

If you think that there are useful COPs within your firm, you may want to support them by identifying a community coordinator, who could:

- identify the business need that the COP supports;
- inform the rest of the firm about the COP and how it helps the business;
- ask some to make specific contributions;
- arrange a few core meetings and introduce people;
- make notes at meetings and post documents on their discussion boards

If you would like to read more about communities of practice, there is additional reading listed at Appendix 2.

After action learning

After action learning (AAL) was introduced by the US army to learn the lessons of engagements, both successful and unsuccessful. It is based around four simple questions:

1. What was supposed to happen?
2. What actually happened?
3. What worked well?
4. What didn't work well?

AAL in the legal field is nothing new either. David Maister has talked about systematic debriefing of engagements since 1999.[10] In principle most fee earners would agree that a valuable amount of learning happens during engagements for clients. This isn't simply learning about technical law, although there is usually plenty of knowledge to add to precedents and practice notes, but also systems learning about how best to manage the workflow and plenty of client-related learning about how this client likes to work and what their industry sector is concerned about at present. And plenty of valuable tacit knowledge learnt by those involved in the matter.

Given that all those involved in practice management understand how important it is to keep existing clients happy and learn about their sector in order to expand the firm's offerings to new clients, why is AAL not successfully entrenched in all law firms, large and small? It probably relates back to the fundamental way that all fee earners are measured and valued by their firms: the chargeable hour target. Actions such as AAL are non-chargeable and so get 'postponed'. Secondly, fee earners are human, and there is always a sense of anticipation about a new matter with all its potential to be interesting and valuable, and the sense of relief that the one you have just finished is over, with a tinge of disappointment that perhaps you weren't always perfect in your management of it. Who would rather rake over past problems in return for non-chargeable time, instead of starting new exciting projects with plenty of chargeable units?

If a law firm could make a system that effectively learned and shared the lessons from each matter, filtering them through to precedents, practice notes, workflows, training sessions, client information and sector intelligence for marketing purposes, it would steal a march on its competitors.

If you want to make an AAL system that works for your firm, how could you go about it? It may be tempting to design a form for fee earners to fill in but many firms who have tried this have found that the form simply gets ignored, or if it does get completed, it is done half-heartedly and then added to the file, not read or disseminated, or passed to another fee earner who does nothing with it.

If a form-based approach works best for your firm, consider using multiple sections on the form or multiple forms for lessons in different areas (client intelligence, market intelligence, changes to precedents, workflows and practice notes, training ideas) and including completion of your form in your pre-file closure system, so that a fee earner can't send out a final bill or archive the file until this is finished. Also, enlist help from non-fee earning staff, so that once the relevant staff have drawn out the lessons learned, the administration of sharing that amongst the right people gets passed on to those without chargeable time targets.

If you opt for a meetings-based discussion system, you will need to schedule regular debriefing meetings, or include them in training meetings. Face-to-face meetings can transmit more information through tone, inflexion, body language, questioning to drill down reasoning, etc., but only if the firm has a particularly supportive culture.

Whether you opt for a paper-based/codification system or a meetings-based/discussion system, the important aspects are to ensure that:

- the right, valuable information gets extracted from the matter;
- the lessons learned get fed into the right people and into the right systems;
- practices are changed as a result of the data;
- longer term problems or lessons are drawn out from a series of AALs.

To make the system work, you will need a non-judgemental atmosphere which encourages sharing of bad decisions and experiences as well as the good, easy to say but difficult to implement. For more ideas about improving your firm's knowledge-sharing culture, see Chapter 5.

Know-who, not just know-how: connecting people

Expert databases and internal White Pages

One excellent way to facilitate the connection of people is to develop a corporate White Pages or database of internal expertise.[11] For this to be a worthwhile project for knowledge-sharing, the database must contain not only contact information, but reliable information about expertise, which must be searchable by topic of expertise.

Again, to be successful there must be a level of trust: for the users, that the information about expertise is reliable and up to date (no one wants an inexpert expert); and for the volunteers, that they won't be taken advantage of as a result of being listed as an expert.

In order to ensure that only true experts are listed under each topic, not over-ambitious juniors, a firm will need to have central control over managing the list. The types of factors that a firm could use to determine who is a true expert could be:

- Publications (books, articles).
- Training courses undertaken or given.
- Work undertaken, successful transactions or cases.
- Membership of specialist groups.
- Entries in legal directories.
- Areas of interest, internal or external.
- Experience with previous employers.
- Peer review.

In order to develop a White Pages of experts within a firm, you will need to gather the following information[12] from them in order to build their profiles:

1. What are your core areas of expertise?
2. Which projects/major cases have you worked on?
3. Have you published articles this year (in internal newsletters or external publications)?
4. Where have you previously worked?

5. Have you changed career or do you have any different areas of expertise (engineering, medicine, etc.)?
6. What training courses have you attended in the last year?
7. What areas are you interested in, but are not currently working on?
8. Which two particular aspects would you grade yourself as an expert?

As well as self-reported expertise, it could be helpful to take into account Belbin roles:[13]

1. Action-oriented roles – shaper, implementer and completer/finisher.
2. People-oriented roles – coordinator, team worker and resource investigator.
3. Cerebral roles – plant, monitor evaluator and specialist.

The difficulty with these databases, whether online or on paper, is that they become stale as soon as they are published. They must be kept up to date to keep their value and to keep trust in their contents. Often a firm will hold this kind of information within the human resources (HR) department, so the database could be jointly created with HR, or linked to their system. Also, a system could be set up to remind fee earners to check and complete their profiles, perhaps before appraisal time, when they are naturally reviewing what they have done throughout the year and they are motivated.

There are expertise-profiling software packages, which look at things like document creation, internet browsing behaviour and track online community activity, such as posting on discussion boards, but unless your firm is large, this is unlikely to be worth the cost.

Knowledge fairs

Another means of connecting people so that they know who to approach in the future, which has gained in popularity recently with larger accountancy and consultancy firms, is the 'knowledge fair'. Run like a market, there may be stalls of some sort setting out what different groups do, or it may be less formal. The important aspect is to ensure that there are no set preconceptions about who should talk to whom about what, so that staff can make new contacts. These have the benefit of both an element of serendipity and sufficient organisation for those looking for a specific person or solution to find them. If it is organised like a conference with little down-time, the benefits will be fewer. In fact many people will say how much they enjoyed the lunch or coffee at a conference and how they made useful contacts, rather than discuss the content of the conference itself.

The benefits of knowledge fairs can be replicated on a smaller scale in law firms by creating locations and occasions for staff to interact, either more formally, such as the Japanese talk rooms, or informally, such as team lunches, annual picnics. Lawyers, due to the nature of their training and the focus on chargeable time as a productivity measure, are unlikely to immediately value informal knowledge-sharing, so a firm may wish to concentrate on the more formal aspects (knowledge fair, an 'ask-the-expert' coffee morning, attendance at conferences) and gradually add the informal ones.

When deciding how to share valuable tacit knowledge within your firm, look at the possible ways (White Pages, collaborative worksites) and choose those which suit your firm.

Summary: the least you need to know

- Tacit knowledge is subjective insight and experience.
- It is difficult to share tacit knowledge through codification, but it can be shared online through storytelling, supporting communities of practice and after action learning.
- Firms can help to connect the right people by preparing an expert database or corporate white pages, searchable by expertise.
- Tacit knowledge is most effectively shared through conversation, especially face-to-face meetings. A firm could try:

  – knowledge fairs;
  – ask an expert coffee mornings or talk rooms;
  – mentoring.

ANNEX 6A: Project idea – run a Gurteen knowledge cafe

What are they?

Developed by David Gurteen, a knowledge cafe is, according to his website, a 'means of bringing a group of people together to have an open, creative conversation on a topic of mutual interest to surface their collective knowledge, to share ideas and insights and to gain a deeper understanding of the subject and the issues involved. This ultimately, leads to action in the form of better decision making and innovation and thus tangible business outcomes.'

There is no set format, but the following is suggested by David Gurteen:

- Facilitator welcomes participants.
- Facilitator sets out the question for the session and raises some brief ideas. This is not a traditional PowerPoint presentation. This should take around 10–15 minutes.
- The group divides into smaller groups of about five to discuss the issue. No attempt is made to capture the conversation at this stage, as this tends to inhibit or slow the discussion. This should take around 45 minutes. If appropriate, participants could swap seats to join different discussions at a set point.

What are they for?

The purpose of the knowledge cafe format is to:

- Facilitate discussion.
- Innovate/surface new ideas and new understanding through open discussion.

When are they useful?

Getting to the root cause of complex business problems in a non-confrontational way:

- Training and learning – especially sharing tacit knowledge.
- Devising high level strategies.
- Connecting people, developing networks, improving relationships and knowledge-sharing cultures.
- Listening within organisations, so employees feel engaged.

How to get started.

These can be low cost events. You will need:

- a facilitator who understands the concept;
- a room or rooms set out with groups of chairs/tables.

Where to find out more information.

- *Internet resources:* **www.gurteen.com**.
- *Training events:* David Gurteen runs regular masterclasses in London and abroad about setting up knowledge cafes. The details of these are on his website. There are knowledge cafes run in many major towns. Many are free to attend and after office hours.

- *Experience one:* The topics discussed may not be of particular interest to lawyers, but it will be useful to experience the format.

ANNEX 6B: **Top tips for using blogs, wikis, social media and online communities of practice**

Ten 'Do's'

1. Use it with the right groups – the following factors all affect whether the group will use the technology or not

    - Size and cohesiveness (trust is a big issue).
    - Technical expertise, experience and enthusiasm.
    - Politics, culture and personalities. (Do people share already? Are they supportive of each other?)
    - Privacy concerns – need to be addressed and the group may need to be updated about the relevant security levels of email and your system.

2. Use it for the right purpose – focus on a key problem that needs to be solved, which offers a tangible benefit and sell that benefit to the potential users.

3. Focus on ease of use:

    - Offer guidance for use, rather than inflexible page templates.
    - Respond flexibly if the community starts to use the technology in different ways.

4. Use the right content:

    - Integrate with other technologies (RSS feeds, email) as far as possible for maximum population for minimum effort (provided it is useful content).
    - Keep it useful and trustworthy – when people see the benefits they will use the technology.

5. Encourage contributions:

    - Encourage junior members of staff to contribute.
    - Respond positively to those who contribute, don't just accept their contributions.
    - Have an on-going programme of reminders to staff and training about its usefulness and how to use it.
    - Use the personal touch – keep language friendly and avoid a 'corporate' tone on blogs.

6. Keep it trustworthy:

    - Fix links and typos.

7. Get people comfortable with it:

    - Avoid technical language.

- Get people started with something they are comfortable with, this could be a personal page, or a short Q&A/top tips article on a topic they know well.
- Get people to use the wiki regularly, perhaps by including agendas for relevant meetings there for people to discuss the meeting beforehand.

8. Let people choose roles that suit them:

- Some may suit the 'gardening' i.e. fixing links and typos, adding references and quotations.
- Others may suit a 'champion' role – encouraging its use by others.

9. Once you have one or two successful groups, start to roll the programme out, using the first groups as mentors and champions.
10. Measure your success.

Five 'Don't's

1. Assume that once you have built it, they will come – these always take time to get off the ground, don't get disheartened.
2. Assume that one training session in 'how to use it' will be enough – plan a programme of different types of training (group, individual, desk-based, team-based) on an ongoing basis.
3. Control it too much – the biggest problem you will face is likely to be that not enough people contribute and people only contribute their absolute highest quality, not that you have too much or inappropriate material.
4. Forget to include a private place for people to draft their blog posts before publishing them.
5. Think that you are creating or have to create Wikipedia – your business needs are different, respond to those business needs.

ANNEX 6C: Project idea – try an ask-an-expert coffee morning

I first came across this idea when preparing to present at an Ark conference with a PSL from Allen & Overy. She had set up an 'ask an expert' coffee morning which had become a great success with the fee earners, who found that it filled a gap between discussions with peers and their personal network, and formal supervision.

The idea is very simple: once a week, or whenever suits your team/department/firm, you take over a room in your offices, provide coffee and biscuits and encourage approachable senior-junior fee earners and partners to hang around for an hour or so, be available to answer questions on matters and generally talk about work to those who need some friendly help.

The informality of the situation encourages knowledge sharing through case-study sharing (storytelling) and conversation, without the pressure and fear of failure that can affect supervisory relationships.

If you want to, you can also use these coffee mornings to improve internal networking and cross selling by including fee earners from other departments/teams, which may also improve knowledge creation and sharing by bringing a different perspective to problems.

Firms may worry that time which could have been spent fee earning will be wasted, but discussions about files and supervision are chargeable and if the solution reached through collaboration is more elegant through these discussions, then the client will be delighted and if not, the time may be written off the final bill, but the benefit of improved networks and the sharing of tacit knowledge will remain.

In a lot of ways, this is like the talk rooms of the Japanese businesses, repurposed for law firms.

Endnotes

1 Dorothy Leonard-Barton, author of *Wellsprings of Knowledge*, HBSP (1998), believes that 80% of the important knowledge in an organisation is tacit and resists codification.

2 Webber, A. (1993) 'What's so new about the new economy' *Harvard Business Review* Jan-Feb, 27.

3 Davenport, T. and Prusak, L. (2000) *Working Knowledge*, Harvard Business School Press, p. 92.

4 See Annex 6C for a project idea.

5 This case study is from Rumizen, M. (2002) *The Complete Idiot's Guide to Knowledge Management*, CWL Publishing Enterprises, p. 108.

6 Emint (**www.emint.org.uk**) is a specialist collaboration forum for people who manage online communities. It recommends at least five loud voices (experts or gurus) and 30 active voices for each loud voice. Many firms won't have these numbers of fee earners, but will still gain value from collaboration tools. The important factor is to ensure that there are sufficient noticeably involved experts to build trust in the users.

7 Weick, K. (1995) *Sensemaking in Organisations*, Sage Publications, p. 127 via Davenport and Prusak (2000), p. 81.

8 Etienne Wenger is credited with creating the term 'community of practice', although he shares credit with Jean Laval, a former colleague.

9 Annex 6B gives some ideas how to support these groups using these social ICT tools.

10 Maister, D. (2003) *Managing the Professional Services Firm*, Simon & Schuster UK Ltd, p. 363.

11 There is more information about expert databases, knowledge maps and social network analysis in Annex 5A.

12 Chaffey, D. and Wood, S. (2005) *Business Information Management*, Pearson Education Ltd. p. 237.

13 Belbin, M. (2003) *Belbin team roles*. Available at **www.belbin.com** (accessed 10 April 2012) as reported in Chaffey and Wood (2005), p. 238.

Chapter 7

Training and learning

After reading this chapter you should appreciate:

- How lawyers learn

- The importance of reflective learning

- How to develop a training schedule

- How to improve trainers' skills

and have a few new ideas to improve the training in your firm.

The cornerstone of a firm's knowledge development and sharing strategy is its training programme. This handbook is not a psychology textbook and cannot give you an exhaustive explanation of learning theories, but this chapter aims to explain in simple terms how lawyers learn, how good training programmes can be put together, what skills trainers need to develop, and to give you a few ideas to try out in order to find the right training plan for your firm.

Why invest in training?

Training is expensive. It can be time-consuming to arrange internal training and costly to buy in training from external providers. It takes fee earners away from earning fees. Training is, however, supremely important for practising lawyers.

Clients can access a vast sea of information themselves on the internet and they expect as a minimum that their lawyers will be up to date. In fact most clients, when instructing a lawyer, are expecting to buy the combined package of the lawyer's experience (the tacit knowledge) in addition to the explicit knowledge. If lawyers are not sufficiently up to date with the law, clients will quickly look elsewhere and professional negligence claims may also mount.

If training is basic but lacklustre, a firm may survive the negligence claims and keep its loyal clients, but it will struggle to win new clients and will gradually lose its talented lawyers. This may be a slower death, but it is a death sentence nonetheless.

This fundamental fact, coupled with increasing anecdotal reports of law students starting their training contracts without sufficient understanding of legal research basics, in particular, a lack of understanding of the hierarchies of value of different source materials, being primarily used to Googling and Westlaw, means that a firm's training programme is of the utmost importance.

How do people learn?

You, the reader, will have already been taught vast amounts. You probably have a degree and a professional qualification, and perhaps a Masters as well. How did you learn the knowledge needed for these and how did you learn to do your job when a newly qualified graduate? You probably have some recollection of revision techniques you were taught, something about different types of learners using visual or audio aids, something about repetition and practice, and maybe also something similar to the medical profession's 'See one, do one, teach one'. The many theories of learning cannot be covered in a handbook like this one, but two theories which emerged in the mid 1980s will be explained: Kolb's 'learning cycle' which approaches learning from a teaching perspective, and Nonaka and Takeuchi's 'knowledge spiral', which approaches learning from a knowledge management perspective.

The learning cycle

In 1984, Kolb, Rubin and MacIntyre developed a simple framework to explain how people learn, using an integration of theory and experience.[1] They viewed learning as a circular process.

Experience is followed by reflection and conceptualisation, which makes sense of that experience. Experimentation with the concepts developed as a result follows, which is, in turn, followed by further experiences, reflection, etc.

Kolb's theory posits that learning is an active process. Experience or theoretical knowledge alone is insufficient. Learners must reflect on what they have been told, understand it, experiment based upon it and learn ways of doing things better based on that theoretical knowledge and experience.

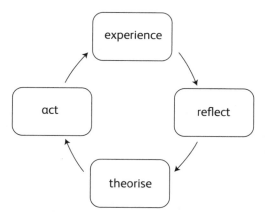

Figure 7.1 The learning cycle

The knowledge spiral

The knowledge spiral is explained in detail in Chapter 2. Referring back to Figure 2.3 you will see from the diagram that the knowledge spiral is similar to Kolb's knowledge cycle, but with a focus on knowledge creation, distribution and transfer across an organisation, rather than an individual's learning method.

Kolb's learning cycle and Nonaka's knowledge spiral teach us three key fundamental problems with many firms' training programmes:

1. Both cycles emphasise the importance of connections between people and learning as an active process, through experience. More IT is rarely the answer to a firm's knowledge-sharing and training-related problems.
2. Only one quadrant in Kolb's learning cycle encompasses the traditional 'chalk and talk' training method.
3. Reflection to assimilate what has been taught is an important part of both cycles.

A firm which addresses these three points in planning and developing its training programme ought to have a clear head start against its competitors.

Devising a training programme

When devising a whole firm training programme, the knowledge spiral or knowledge cycle are good places to start. A firm could purchase an external providers' information, make it available to lawyers and leave them to it, but even if it incentivised them strongly to self-teach (unlikely unless their chargeable time targets were cut drastically), the result would still only be part-trained lawyers, who were missing the key 'value-add'.

The best training programmes include aspects from the entire knowledge spiral, i.e. include the following:

- **socialisation** – on-the-job training, mentoring, supervision, discussions (peer-to-peer or facilitated, knowledge cafes), assisted communities of practice (online (wikis, discussion boards, blogs) or in person (informal meetings and discussions));
- **externalisation** – lectures and discussion groups (formal and informal, in person or online, interactive or videos);
- **combination** – written information in databases or on paper; and
- **internalisation** – opportunities for reflection and internalisation.

Reflective learning/internalisation is an extremely important part of the learning cycle and knowledge spiral, but one that is often overlooked by law firms. Unless a lawyer is extremely disciplined or has a low chargeable time target, he/she is unlikely to find many spare hours to quietly 'reflect' on what he/she has learnt and many may be suspicious of something so 'soft' or which suggests a management fad. It is likely, therefore, that some form of encouraged, coerced or mandatory reflective learning, supported by incentives, will be required in a training programme, perhaps couched as a learning log which must be discussed at appraisal to check adherence to continuous professional development (CPD) requirements.

Reflective learning itself is not always a comfortable experience. People tend to be protective of their identities and many lawyers' identities as 'expert lawyers' may be questioned by these reflections, but they are essential. A private learning log as well as a public/shared one may suit a firm, depending upon its culture.

Some form of 'after action learning' (AAL) is a simple way to systematise post-transaction reflective learning: this could be as simple as a four-question form such as that used by the US army (see Box 7.1) or a more detailed questionnaire (see Box 7.2).

Staff who become mentors or supervisors, who teach in some format, whether internal training sessions or client seminars, or who write articles for in-house magazines, firm newsletters or for external publishers, engage naturally in reflective learning and often find the experience enhances their own working practices as well as that of their students, mentees and readers.

Online tests, where there are opportunities to revisit what has been learned and mull over what has been understood and where gaps still remain, can also encourage reflective learning. How reflective learning is best conducted will depend upon what was taught, how it was taught and who was learning, coupled with the overall culture of the business.

BOX 7.1   After action learning US army-style

1.   What was supposed to happen?
2.   What actually happened?
3.   What worked well?
4.   What didn't work well?

US army-style AAL amounts to 15 words and four simple questions, but its simplicity disguises a learning system that can return vast amounts of reflective learning.
   To make the system work for you, you will need:

- a non-judgemental atmosphere which encourages sharing of bad decisions and experiences as well as the good;
- to act on the information received, not just collect it:
  - to share it as appropriate and in a manner which is appropriate,
  - to draw out longer term problems or benefits from one-offs, and
  - to change practices as a result of the data.

AAL can be a simple single transaction/matter review, or it can encompass multiple transactions, drawing out long-term issues or learning points, although law firms must always be wary of the level of cost of this kind against the benefit from analysing the data.

BOX 7.2   Questions for private learning logs

How did that go?
How did I feel about the experience? Why did I feel that way?
What did I learn from it?
What did I fail to learn?
How might I have acted more effectively?
What will I do differently as a result, to help me learn better?

Tools

Reflections can be captured in written format (notebooks), online (blogs) or as audio diaries.
   Feedback from others can be useful, although not if it inhibits honest reflection.

Devising the training sessions

When devising the nuts and bolts of each training session, it is helpful to begin with the following questions, then work backwards devising the session around the answers:

1. Who is learning? Who is the audience?
2. What are their learning needs?
3. What is the objective of this learning session?
4. What do the answers to these questions mean for the practicalities of preparing this training session?

Who is learning?

The audience for a firm-wide technical legal training programme may cover newly qualified solicitors, perhaps paralegals or trainees if a firm has any, and experienced senior lawyers. Support staff will also need specialist training and support, although this isn't covered in this handbook. Each of these professional groups will have very different needs, each of which will have to be addressed.

Looking at all lawyers as a group, it can be helpful when addressing their training needs in technical law, to understand a bit more about them and their typical personalities.

There has been a surprising amount of research into the types of people who become lawyers and which personalities make successful lawyers. Professor Susan Daicoff, Professor of Law at Florida Coastal School of Law and visiting law professor at other universities, explained her research in her book *Lawyer, Know Thyself*.[2] In general terms, she found that lawyers are:

- argumentative, dominant and aggressive;
- have a low interest in people and less humanitarianism;
- have a greater than normal incidence of psychological distress and substance abuse; and
- have a preference for Myers-Briggs INTJ (Intuitive, Introverts, Thinkers, Judgers), which means that they:[3]

  - have original minds;
  - have a great drive for implementing their ideas and achieving their goals;
  - quickly see patterns in external events and develop long-range explanatory perspectives;
  - when committed, organise a job and carry it through;
  - are sceptical and independent;
  - have high standards of competence and performance – for themselves and others.

That may not sound like a great recipe to tempt anyone to present lectures to them, but this personality type enables them to give advice and representation to all kinds of clients, including those whom they may dislike or disapprove of.

Training sessions will be easier if these group traits are taken into account. In particular:

- As introverts, lawyers will need a little time to mull over their thoughts on topics before contributing at a useful, deeper level at a meeting or training session, so circulate details of the training topic in advance. This can become a problem when the training sessions are regular and lawyers begin to simply turn up to listen, without knowing in advance what the topic is.

- Lawyers can be argumentative, so trainers or speakers will need to be:

  - well-prepared, and warned not to take any arguments personally;
  - ready and confident enough to manage any arguments that begin to take the session off-topic.

- Given the levels of expertise within a firm, the hierarchical nature of the law firm, and the regular discussions and arguments, some lawyers can be wary of superior/peer disapproval and underestimate their levels of expertise, which means they can be reticent in raising genuine questions, as they fear that these may be judged as ill-thought out. This problem can be overcome in a number of ways, including:

  - training different levels of expertise at different sessions;
  - encouraging discussions by 'planting' a few questions with friendly fee earners to get the discussions started;
  - general tone and using facilitation techniques; and
  - using simple 'hands in the air' voting before the session and after.

At first glance, lawyers' innate traits do not seem to be those which encourage open discussions and nuanced learning, but once these are understood and taken into account in planning training sessions, the quality of training can be improved immensely.

What are the group's learning needs?

The firm's needs in training its lawyers may be to:

1. minimise professional negligence claims;
2. maximise client satisfaction with existing work;
3. develop areas of expertise in new or existing areas of work and/or develop new legal products to sell; or
4. maximise the satisfaction of its lawyers, so that it does not lose its talent.

Where a firm is concentrating its efforts on goal 1, it will need to begin with a basic job description of each role and understand the basic levels of expertise necessary for that role. Existing lawyers should be able to identify these levels and each newcomer to the department should be fully versed in what is expected at a basic level. If there are sufficient funds, it may be easier to outsource these fundamental training needs to an external source, as there are many such courses available across the country, but if not, the firm's lawyers should be able to offer these sessions.

In some ways, the first goal is probably the easiest to fulfil. The other goals are more nuanced, but each department's existing lawyers ought to know what the training needs of the department are. They may not know all the different and most productive ways to fulfil those needs, but they will know what it is that they need to know in order to do their jobs, and what gaps their near-misses have identified. A small focus group of fee earners is an ideal way to devise the content for at least 50 per cent of a department's technical training (emailing the whole department rarely returns any significant insights).

One training need that is often overlooked, and so is a great opportunity for firms, is the training needs of senior lawyers, in particular to develop new areas of expertise or develop new products. A firm which addresses this need ought to find itself ahead of its competitors quite quickly. In this situation, as well as taking advice from senior lawyers, it is a good idea to consult clients as to their needs.

Feedback from tenders can be a good starting-point. What were the presenters quizzed about? What did the clients seem interested in? What went well; what went badly? Also, if a firm takes client feedback regularly, this can be fed into the training schedule: what do clients wish the firm did better, what services do they wish the firm would add to its portfolio of services? For more information, see Chapter 8 and especially Annex 8A.

Also, a firm can study the AAL points. What are lawyers getting wrong? What do they wish they had done better?

Of course, different levels of expertise within each speciality will need different training sessions: different topics and different methods of delivery. To overcome this, a firm can train different levels of lawyers separately, which has the added benefit of improving engagement by more junior lawyers. Targeted training sessions often get better buy-in and attendance levels from staff, who can see that none of their precious time is being wasted. However, these targeted sessions must be mixed with sessions which include all levels of expertise. Mixed sessions are needed to cascade knowledge informally through discussion, from partners to juniors, but in this situation the partners will need to know in advance that that is the purpose of the session and that they will be judged by how inclusively and non-judgementally they offer their experiences. Mixed sessions could also use a magazine format, with 20 minutes on a couple of different topics, each aimed at a different level. The important questions to ask of each session are 'What is this session for?' and 'Who is it for?'

What is the objective of the training session?

Before deciding what method of training/learning is the best one to deliver the group's needs, it is necessary to understand the objective of the training. Despite the nature of how CPD is measured, it is important to focus on the outputs required by the firm, not just the time spent.

If a firm is offering technical legal training to develop expertise in an existing area of work, it may be tempting to only offer a programme of 'chalk and talk' over lunchtimes. It is difficult to teach a technical subject so that lawyers learn and retain information in a one-hour lunchtime slot, but it is possible for that session to signpost an issue and teach lawyers where to find suitable information for the future, also to highlight who is an expert in that field, for more nuanced questions and future discussions.

Preparing a training programme – the practicalities

Once the audience, their training needs and the training session's objective have been considered, many of the practicalities of how to deliver the programme will become apparent.

There are many different ways of offering training; each has its own best-fit for a particular audience or particular objective.

Whilst it may be tempting for the sake of efficiency to develop packs of written information for lawyers to absorb or to offer them reading lists, oral communication is thought to be more effective than written communication in conveying meaning, so the majority of sessions will require attendance at an orally presented session. This does not mean that they need to be dry 'chalk and talk' lectures. Narrative and drama can convey complex messages very effectively. Lawyers naturally use this technique when explaining technical law by way of case studies. Lectures can also be followed by Q&A sessions and discussions in large and small groups. Another good learning session could be by way of current case discussions: one lawyer is chosen to bring a particularly knotty problem to a discussion group. Smaller, supportive groups work best. These groups can either discuss a problem that has already been resolved (either well or badly, depending upon how supportive the group is), looking for neater solutions, or a current problem that needs a solution. How useful these groups are depends very much on the culture of the business: how accepting the culture is of mistakes; how open lawyers are about gaps in their knowledge; and how open lawyers are to others' suggestions.

To minimise cost there is no need to use external or internal speakers for each training session in order to keep interest in the programme. Many different webinars are available and value can be added by watching the webinar in a group, then discussing the issues in more depth, perhaps with a case study to work through.

More ideas to improve technical training can be found in Box 7.3 below.

BOX 7.3   Ideas to improve technical training sessions

- Make them easy to attend, which usually means that they need to be regular and at lunchtime. If you can afford to offer lunch, all the better.
- Training sessions need not be compulsory, but it is important to engage all staff at some point. Expert lawyers may not need technical training themselves, but they will be needed to pass on their expertise during discussions and will benefit from networking opportunities.
- Where possible, mix lawyers from different departments, so that sessions also act as a networking opportunity.
- If getting discussions started is difficult, prime a few friendly lawyers with pre-planned questions.
- Leave each participant with a:
    - 'least you need to know' sheet;
    - list of suitable resources and precedents;
    - list of 'experts' within the firm (both senior partners for complex questions and junior staff for those 'stupid' questions everyone has).
- Capture the training sessions in whatever ways you can and create a montage, so they can be viewed at a later date for revision or for those who were unable to attend. You could use:
    - film, audio files, photographs of flipchart notes, slides with notes or audio attached, diagrams, mind-maps or whatever suits the training session and the attendees;
    - these could be put online, kept on paper at the library or in the department, or put on a notice board, perhaps near the coffee machine or water cooler.
- Always build in a means of reflection to each session. This may be as simple as a reminder to complete a learning log, an online test or a follow-up discussion session (see below).

After the training session

Reflective learning and getting maximum benefit from knowledge created/shared

Once a session has been delivered, make sure that training materials are easily accessible for those who want to review them and those who missed the session, and make maximum use of the knowledge that has been created and shared in the session.

Ensure that all individuals are encouraged to undertake some form of reflective learning. If your lawyers dislike jargon, call it a debrief. This could be completing an online test or filling in a learning log. It could be a second discussion session or it could be by way of writing or teaching about the topic. Reusing knowledge in other ways, such as creating articles for the firm's newsletter, articles for external publication or client seminars, minimises the non-chargeable time spent on these marketing needs and ensures good quality by basing them on group input. Volunteers could be taken at the end of each training session.

From a business viewpoint, a post-training session is a good time for a quick review of job descriptions, competencies for each grade, and intranet knowledge packs to ensure they are up to date.

Post-training sessions are also a good time to encourage lawyers to become more involved in teaching, whether that is internal training sessions, mentoring and supervising, client seminars, or teaching at higher education level. Teaching has multiple benefits. At a basic level, it helps to connect staff to a more diverse group. It also forces lawyers to prioritise learning, to learn to explain something complex in simple terms and to orientate a subject within a wider picture. It provides the motivation for in-depth preparation and encourages a lawyer to divide out core and supplementary learning. Lastly, it enables lawyers to become expert in a topic, which improves their internal network and external reputation.

Get feedback to improve future sessions

As well as attendees reflecting on the content of the training session, it is important for the trainer to reflect on the success or otherwise of the session itself, and to get feedback from attendees in order to improve the next sessions.

Donald Kirkpatrick, Emeritus Professor of the University of Wisconsin and a past president of the American Society for Training and Development, has developed a four-level evaluation programme in his book 'Evaluating Training Programmes'.[4] In simplistic terms he suggests studying:

1. **reaction** – to what degree participants reacted favourably to the training;
2. **learning** – to what degree participants acquired the intended knowledge, skills, attitudes, confidence and commitment based on their participation in a training event;
3. **behaviour** – to what degree participants later apply what they learned during training when they are back on the job; and
4. **results** – to what degree targeted outcomes occurred as a result of the training event and subsequent reinforcement.

Ideally, as each training session is being developed, and the first three questions ('Who is learning', 'What are their learning needs?' and 'What is the objective of this learning session?') are being considered, a firm will also bear in mind how to meet these four levels.

Donald Kirkpatrick warns[5] that without working on all four levels, learning professionals put most of their resources into the part of the training process that produces the lowest level of business results: the training session itself. They spend relatively little time in the pre-training preparation and follow-up activities that translate into positive behaviour change and subsequent results (Levels 3 and 4).

Lastly, but most importantly, the results from this evaluation must be fed back into the overall training programme in order to continuously improve it.

In smaller firms this level of evaluation may seem like overkill, but where training budgets are tight, it is more important than ever that money is spent wisely, and of course, once an evaluation form has been created that suits a firm, it can be reused and/or adapted easily.

Improving trainers' skills

The last section in this chapter is an overview of some of the ways that a firm can support its trainers to improve their skills. Some people are more naturally adept at training than others, but even those who find training difficult can improve their skills. There are a number of good 'train the trainer' courses available, so if a firm is planning that one person should present the majority of its in-house training, it will probably be cost-effective to pay for that person to attend these courses, or join with other local firms to have some bespoke local training. If, however, that cost isn't warranted, this section will give a few ideas for those undertaking training events to improve retention of knowledge amongst their audience. There is also plenty of additional reading listed at the end of the book and Annex 7A contains ideas to improve a presenter's PowerPoint skills.

Before beginning the session, the trainer should make sure the room is set up appropriately to the session. Would it suit a lecture style or groups? Is it the right temperature and are the right tools available? Is the presentation correctly loaded and does he/she know how to use that room's technology?

Once attendees have arrived, but before the training session starts, a presenter will want to improve rapport with the group. Ice-breaker games can fall flat with some lawyers, but time spent chatting informally with the attendees before starting the session itself works well, as do informal quizzes, shows of hands, etc.

When giving the session, the trainer can improve engagement by:

- using a mix of media – PowerPoint, flipcharts, whiteboards;
- using a mix of engagement levels – lecturing, quizzes, discussions;

- dividing information down into chunks, using mnemonics and repetition of key phrases to improve retention;
- using all the audience's senses – visual aids, sound files, props;
- being aware if the audience's energy level wanes and using a change of topic, media or level of engagement to re-energise the group.

It is also advisable that all presenters practise dealing with fielding questions. They will need to ensure equal opportunities for the whole audience to discuss the issues, deal with relevant questions simply, but shut down unhelpful arguments or off-topic discussions, and sometimes redirect questions back to the room, becoming more of a facilitator than trainer.

Lastly, a trainer must ensure that appropriate post-session materials are given to all attendees, giving a summary of what has been discussed, details of where to find out more information and something to encourage post-session reflective learning and, if a trainer hopes to continuously improve, a feedback form for immediate completion.

BOX 7.4   Presentation skills: voice and body language

Voice skills

- speak at an even pace
- vary tone, volume and inflection to emphasise key aspects
- use pauses

Body language

- avoid irritating gestures (video your presentations to discover them)
- practise an open and confident stance and moving with energy and grace
- ensure gestures are inclusive of the audience
- make eye contact with the whole of the group throughout the session, but do not stare

---

Summary: the least you should know

How lawyers learn

There are a number of theories of learning, but this handbook recommends that the reader takes into account Kolb's learning cycle and/or Nonaka's knowledge spiral when devising training schedules, ensuring that the schedule as a whole provides for all four quadrants of learning. Research suggests that lawyers have a distinct personality type and it is recommended that this too is taken into account.

The importance of reflective learning

Both the learning cycle and knowledge spiral include a reflective phase, which is often forgotten when devising training for lawyers. It is difficult for lawyers to make time to reflect upon their training, but there are techniques to encourage reflection, the most efficient of which is a combination of reusing training in client seminars and for articles, coupled with learning logs (private and open) which are discussed at appraisals.

How to develop a training schedule

When devising a training schedule, it is important to bear in mind who the audience is, what their learning needs are and the outputs required from the training, and then developing each session to fit those requirements.

How to improve trainers' skills

Trainers can improve engagement with their audience by building rapport at the outset, mixing training styles and media to keep interest going, and working on their voice and body language skills.

ANNEX 7A: Improve your PowerPoint presentations

Like it or loathe it, many people in the legal sector use PowerPoint for their presentations. But how often do you hear people moaning about them? It can be a useful tool, or create snooze-inducing talks. Here are five top tips to help you improve your PowerPoint presentations.

1. Remember that any slides you use are supposed to support you, the presenter, not be an end in themselves

You are the most important aspect of the presentation, not the content on the slides. Remember to keep the focus on you. Don't cut the time you ought to be using to practise your presentation in order to perfect the slides.

2. Do you really need to use PowerPoint?

It may be your habit to always reach for PowerPoint when preparing a presentation, but ask yourself whether it is the right medium. Would your point be better made using a whiteboard, a flip chart, a demonstration, or no visual aids at all? Avoid dull PowerPoint presentations by only using PowerPoint when it is the right medium for your talk.

3. Outline

Before you reach for PowerPoint, write an outline for your talk. It will give you a framework and an overall idea of the organisation, chronology and emphasis for your talk.

4. Learn more about PowerPoint

PowerPoint can do more than just list bullet points. You don't want to distract your audience or clutter your slides with whooshing graphics and fancy sound effects, but if you can illustrate your point with a picture or a graph or link through to a live demonstration, people will probably remember your point better. Learning to use PowerPoint is easy, but mastering it takes time. Most firms have someone who could coach you, so find some time to learn more about it.

5. Think like a designer

You may be a lawyer or an information specialist, but spend a little time thinking about the design and look of your slides. They need to be eye catching and interesting, but you need people to concentrate on you and your presentation. Spend some time getting the balance right. It may take a little time at first, but you will soon develop an eye for this. These are some of my thoughts:

- **Limit the amount of information on your slides.** Steve Jobs used to present with only one or two words on his slides (probably not PowerPoint though . . .). There seems to be a general view that people can't take in more than three bits of information on any slide. I have no idea where this has come from, but it seems sensible to limit the amount of information on the slides. I generally try to keep to 3–5 key items. The last thing you want to do is read out large amounts of text from your slides.

- **Choose background design and text to avoid eye strain.** Dark text on a light background is easier on the eye for a long presentation, although light text on dark can be punchy in short ones. Make sure that your text size is large enough and easy to read at a distance.

- **Stay consistent, but choose the appropriate layout for each slide.** You don't want to confuse the eye of your audience, but think about whether you have chosen the right layout for each slide. The title-style slide may suit something midway through your presentation or your point may come across better with several subheading slides.

- **Use the bells and whistles judiciously.** PowerPoint offers all kinds of facilities – importing Excel spreadsheets, clip art, diagrams, photos and links. It is important to know what is available, but remember that the presentation is there to support you and the audience's focus should always be on you. Use the fancy graphics only to enhance your point.

ANNEX 7B: Getting over it – managing presentation nerves

Speaking in public often tops the lists of most feared events and everyone gets nervous beforehand. KM professionals often have to present technical information to tough audiences – KM Heads presenting project proposals to Executive Boards full of Partners, PSLs presenting legal training to a department of lawyers, presentations to KM conferences.

Being well prepared is the obvious first step to minimising presentation nerves. This checklist aims to help improve your presentations, with seven top tips on managing presentation nerves.

1. Be well prepared

Very few people can present well on a topic they know little about, so make sure you are well prepared on the content of your presentation. That goes without saying really. What you may forget to prepare are the practicalities. What technology will be there? Do you need to take your laptop? Will you be standing up or sitting down? What handouts do you need? If there is no lectern or anything similar, what will you do with your notes (and your hands!)? Being confident about these practicalities frees you to concentrate on your talk and take any hitches in your stride. Mark Twain said 'It usually takes me more than three weeks to prepare a good impromptu speech.'

2. Have a back-up plan

Know what you will do if the technology doesn't work or your presentation is in the wrong version of PowerPoint. If you have thought out solutions to potential problems beforehand, you will have less to worry about and in the unlikely event one of the problems occurs, you can impress everyone by taking it in your stride.

3. Visualise

Visualise yourself doing the presentation and it going well. Visualise yourself feeling confident and being clear and competent. You will probably have to do this a number of times for the technique to work. It might feel a bit silly, but professional sports people use visualisation to improve their performance, so why not try it?

4. Run through the presentation beforehand

Don't just look at your slides and think 'and then I'll talk about . . .' actually do a full-scale dummy run and force yourself to think about the actual words you would ideally like to use and say them out loud. Don't memorise your presentation, but do practise it a couple of times. This will also mean you can be confident about timings and you won't run over (and have to put up with people itching to leave) or run out of things to say.

5. Beware of over-practising

It is probably better to over-practise than under practise, but if you run through your presentation too many times it can come across as stilted.

6. Do more presentations

If you fear something, you can desensitise yourself if you do it more often, rather than avoiding it. Choose some safe places to practise i.e. a team meeting or a smaller group or a particularly friendly audience, and get some positive experiences under your belt. I always enjoy presenting to Knowledge Network West because everyone is so interested and positive. Remember that no one likes doing presentations, so your audience is probably more on your side than you think. Also, presenting is a learned skill like any other. You are confident in your day-to-day work because you do it all the time. The more presentations you do, the more you will discover for yourself the skills you need to have an impact and develop your own presentation style.

7. Have a short routine to get you started or to ground you if things start to go wrong

When you stand up to speak, take a minute to breathe in and out, look around the audience, catch the eye of a few friendly faces, smile and then start talking. It connects you to everyone and gives you a minute to calm down. Have a similar routine planned if things feel like they are starting to go wrong. Take a calming breath, look at the current slide, look at the audience, smile while you collect your thoughts and carry on.

Hopefully these seven top tips have given you a few ideas as to how to minimise your presentation nerves. Lastly, always remember: what's the worst that can happen? I don't think the stress of giving a presentation has actually killed anyone yet.

ANNEX 7C: E-learning Q&A with Ann Hemming

What is 'e-learning'?

'E-learning' used to mean an endless run of screens and hitting the next button until the learner got RSI (repetitive strain injury). In its infancy it did get quite a bad reputation, but now technology has moved on, the definition really needs to change to online learning. This term can be used to describe all kinds of learning that is provided using an online medium. This may be a You Tube video, online electronic support; virtual chat, quizzes, formal education programmes, in fact any education delivered online: the list is endless.

E-learning started to become a prominent tool in law firms as part of the IT training portfolio, being a useful way of providing busy lawyers and support staff with self help tools 'just in time'. Now online learning has moved into many areas of business education and the main legal publishers (such as Lexis and PLC) are now offering technical legal training as part of their online portfolio. Online learning is also prepared in-house. Authoring tools have become much more affordable (in some cases free) so it is much easier for a law firm to develop their own in-house online materials for internal (and in some cases external client) consumption.

In-house developed e-learning can be as simple as a videoed presentation by in-house experts on a topic, which is then made available to all, or a library of existing PowerPoint slides enhanced with audio. However some firms are developing quite sophisticated offerings for both their internal audience and as either an additional revenue stream or a value-add service for clients.

E-learning is nothing new. The College of Law and the Open University have both offered video- or TV-based learning for years; however what is exciting now is that development costs have reduced and the options for including e-learning in the firm's portfolio have increased exponentially providing new opportunities to provide afford-able training.

Why should e-learning interest all law firms?

There are a number of key benefits to e-learning, some of which are particularly relevant to middle tier and smaller firms.

E-learning is cost-effective and flexible and offers a means of learning that can adapt to the firm that wants to use it. It avoids wasted travel time and enables firms to train a geographically diverse group simultaneously if it wants to. It is a simple tool that can fit in with the times that fee earners are free, and can be scaled up or down to suit the audience.

It enables topics to be divided into smaller 'chunks', which means that participants are more likely to recall the topics discussed and be able to apply them to their work. This is particularly important for Gen Y learners (who are more used to social media and learning in this way). Firms who want to engage with a younger audience are finding that incorporating online learning helps to keep the generation that does not remember a time before the Internet engaged with training.

Lastly, but importantly, it enables smaller firms to have access to experts that other-wise they could not afford. One of the first webinars that I arranged for Lexis included Lord Neuberger, Master of the Rolls, on the panel. The 'Big Costs Review' Lexis offered in

2011 cost £89 for a two-hour webinar presented by His Honour Michael Cook and Professor Dominic Regan. It is unlikely that a sole costs draftsman would be able to afford to attend a seminar with these experts and interact with them during the seminar, for this cost in their own locality (without wasted travel time).

The Solicitors Regulation Authority (SRA) and other government and regulatory bodies have now embraced the use of technology to make sure that access to education is more fairly distributed and available irrespective of location or size of practice.

All firms are under increased financial pressure and few can afford to maintain the traditional spend on training in times of recession. Training budgets are often (mistakenly in my view) some of the first to be cut when times are bad. However, e-learning can help to spread that budget further, reducing both delivery and lost opportunity costs.

Compliance and risk management are also a prominent part of law firm strategy and e-learning offers the risk management team useful tools to demonstrate compliance. Firms have legal requirements to ensure that their staff have been trained in topics such as Anti Money Laundering, Health and Safety, Anti Bribery and many more. Being able to not only train, but also test and track completion easily online, assists with the demonstration of compliance.

Is interaction not one of the most important aspects of training? How do webinars offer this?

It is a common misconception that e-learning is simply about employees watching videos, webinars or webcasts alone, ticking off their CPD hours. The most effective way to use e-learning is as part of a blended programme of training. It is still important to get groups together to network and share ideas and some types of learning are not suitable for online delivery.

Webinars can be used in a group setting, where all those within a firm who are interested in the topic gather to watch the webinar together, perhaps virtually if they are scattered geographically, then pause the webinar to discuss interesting points together. Discussions could be by video or telephone conference or by social media or a messaging system. It can be useful to have a facilitator to help with the discussions. Where face to face interaction is necessary e-learning can be used both pre and post the face-to-face session to keep sessions focused and timely.

Research has also shown that although there is still a perception that face-to-face learning is more effective than online, this simply is not the case. Bad training is bad training whatever the medium, and the amount of information anyone can take in and retain at one time is quite limited, hence 'chunking' training into shorter more digestible sessions that can be replayed at the learner's convenience is more effective.

How expensive would it be for a firm to set up its own e-learning programme?

It needn't be expensive for a firm to set up its own programme of e-learning. Many tools are free or low-cost and often the skills to develop online learning are no more onerous than learning to use a camera or PowerPoint. Managing and monitoring online learning is also becoming more cost effective. Learning Management Systems used to be prohibitively expensive but now there are excellent open source (free) systems, such as moodle (moodle.org). Alternatively firms can make use of the webinars provided externally, or introduce e-learning gradually using video or telephone conferences, taping (audio or video) existing training to be viewed later, or using social media to facilitate discussions around case reviews. One of the true benefits of e-learning over traditional classroom style training is its flexibility.

What will the future of e-learning look like?

The latest, more sophisticated learning systems can sit behind a user's usual work tools (such as Microsoft software) and offer training 'just in time', to improve drafting. Tools are now being developed that offer clauses and online research and validation as part of the drafting process. Online education will start to become as familiar as the Internet in a very short space of time.

Also, some firms are already beginning to combine many different systems into portals, using technology such as SharePoint. This enables them to provide a 'one stop shop' combining knowledge systems, training, financial information, documents and other external and internal resources all targeted specifically to the user. The move online offers endless possibilities for improving both knowledge management and learning, supporting a more mobile, distributed workforce and a more global legal community. Moreover client demand for online KM and learning tools is growing and that will bring its use to the forefront of firm strategy.

Ann Hemming is Head of KM and L&D (learning and development) at Thomas Eggar LLP; she is also a consultant assisting both law firms and legal publishers to develop effective learning and KM strategies. Ann has worked as a Legal KM and L&D professional for over 25 years.

Endnotes

1   Kolb, D. (1984) *Experiential learning: Experience as the source of learning and development*, Prentice-Hall. Honey, P. and Mumford, A. (1982) *The Manual of Learning Styles*, Peter Honey Publications. Honey, P. and Mumford, A. (1983) *Using Your Learning Styles*, Peter Honey Publications.

2   Daicoff, S. (2004) *Lawyer, Know Thyself: A Psychological Analysis of Personality Strengths and Weaknesses*, American Psychological Association Books.

3   **www.myersbriggs.org/my-mbti-personality-type/mbti-basics/the-16-mbti-types.asp** (accessed 10 April 2012).

4   Kirkpatrick, D. (2006) *Evaluating Training Programs: The Four Levels*, 3rd edn, Berrett-Koehler Publishers.

5   **www.kirkpatrickpartners.com/OurPhilosophy/tabid/66/Default.aspx** (accessed 10 April 2012).

Chapter 8

Client-facing knowledge management

By the end of this chapter you should appreciate:

- What client-facing KM is
- How client-facing KM fits with marketing
- How it helps your clients
- How it helps your firm
- How you can use blogs and Twitter

Introduction

Client-facing KM became the topic *du jour* in the mid 2000s. However, as with many topics discussed in this handbook, this was a new name for an old practice. Law firms have been using knowledge-based marketing for years: quarterly newsletters to clients, publications in journals, seminars to clients. These are all aspects of 'client-facing KM'.

During the first decade of this century there was renewed interest in client-facing KM because of a more coordinated and professional approach to this knowledge-based marketing, and the expansion of offerings as value-added services, partly due to client needs and partly as a result of developments in IT systems. As well as e-newsletters, firms offered extranets with current awareness and useful reference documents and, as firms worked more in partnership with key clients, they offered them the use of their library and information departments and secondments of PSLs.

This handbook concentrates on knowledge management, rather than marketing, but Box 8.1 gives a short guide to the 'least you need to know about marketing' and there is additional suggested reading in Appendix 2.

This chapter will probably appeal more to law firms with business clients, large and small, as it primarily concerns building on-going relationships. Business clients still expect knowledge-based marketing, despite pushing down prices in these recessionary times. This means that firms must work even harder to make maximum use of the content/knowledge that they have and work as smart as they can.

BOX 8.1 Sally Calverley's 'marketing 101'

1. Focus on the customer

   (a) The first rule is: listen to your customer. The second, third and fourth rules are the same.
   (b) The competitive edge in marketing comes from understanding your customers' expectations, wants and needs better than the competition and then doing something about it.
   (c) Design services around clients needs and then explain why the client will benefit from what you have done: clients buy benefits (no more hanging on the phone) not features (we answer the phone in five rings).
   (d) 'Value' and 'Quality' are subjective. Only the client can tell you if they received them – whatever you set out to deliver.
   (e) The fifth rule is: use your expertise to design a solution that meets your clients' needs perfectly. And then repeat as often as required.

2. Marketing is everyone's job

   (a) Create customer focus throughout the business – the client's experience isn't just about the advice, any more than a dinner date is just about the food.
   (b) If opportunities arise where your firm has an existing or potential advantage – go for it. More work is lost through unanswered phones than saying the wrong thing.

3. Only compete in markets where you can establish a competitive advantage

   (a) Define and nurture your firm's distinct competencies, processes or approach. Ask your clients: how are we different?
   (b) Identify resources – perhaps people – that provide customer value AND are hard for competitors to acquire or imitate – then make it harder still.
   (c) Replicate or acquire your competitors' competitive advantage or better still, make it irrelevant.

4. Markets are not homogeneous

   (a) Markets are made up of different individual people, businesses and interest groups. Isn't that wonderful?
   (b) One of the most useful ways for smaller businesses to segment their clients is on the basis of how they measure value.
   (c) Value-based segmentation enables businesses to easily identify targets for new service development or development of growth services.
   (d) Law firms, like accountancy firms, generally struggle with segmentation.

5. Markets and clients are constantly changing

(a) As products and services evolve, clients' expectations increase and patience decreases.

(b) Organisations need to continuously improve their offerings to retain their position.

6. Strategic Customer Management can help to target scarce resources

(a) 20 % of clients may translate into 80 % of profits. Or it may be 10:90!

(b) Large customers aren't always strategic accounts.

(c) It is better to grow existing clients and earn their loyalty, than to constantly chase new clients. Better in the sense of more profitable and less destabilising for the business.

(d) New clients should match the value criteria of clients who love you!

7. It is important to manage for long-term profitability, not short term results

(a) Keeping the 'day to day' running is important.

(b) But having a 'day to day' to worry about next year even more so – so lift your eyes to the horizon.

(c) Ask: will this juicy client help or hinder us in achieving our goals in one, five or ten years?

© Sally Calverley 2012. Sally Calverley is a business and management consultant specialising in advice to professional service firms, especially law firms. She is a director of Richmonte Wells, the client relationship specialist, and also of Cloud Professional Practice, an outsourcing firm for small independent practices.

The key to content marketing, or client-facing KM marketing, is to get the right information in the right way, to the right person and not to waste time, money or effort.

The ideal people to ask what this is, are, of course, the existing clients. An excellent place to start is a RATER survey,[1] an example of which is included at Annex 8A.

Client-facing KM and marketing

In his chapter on attracting new clients, David Maister divided law firm marketing opportunities into three areas: the first team, the second string and the 'clutching at straws' tactics.[2] Although this was first published in 1993 these three areas are as valid as ever. Social media has added to the available channels of communication for connecting with potential clients, but the basic first team remains the same and depends on staff making a personal connection with individuals. Box 8.2 below recreates Maister's list of effective tactics, annotated to include new media.

BOX 8.2   An adapted version of Maister's marketing tactics in descending order of effectiveness

[Author's changes in italics]

The first team

- Seminars (small scale)
- Speeches at client industry meetings
- Articles in client-oriented (trade) press
- Proprietary research
- *Personalised e-newsletters*
- *Blogs (when targeted and used well)*
- *Bespoke training events given to a single client*
- *Inviting key clients to the firm's training events*
- *Newsflash case reports with tailored comments regarding how that case affects each client individually*

The second string

- Community/civic activities
- Networking with potential referral sources
- Newsletters
- *Blogs, general*
- *Twitter (when used well)*
- *LinkedIn groups and discussion boards (when used well)*
- *Podcast training sessions (tailored)*
- *Extranets*

Clutching at straws tactics

- Publicity
- Brochures
- Seminars (ballroom scale)
- Direct mail
- Cold calls
- Sponsorship of cultural/sports events
- Advertising
- Video brochures
- *Syndicated journal articles, such as e-zine*
- *Newsflash case reports (undifferentiated)*
- *Podcasts (general)*
- *Twitter (when used badly)*
- *Facebook (unless your clients are well-represented here and use the site often)*
- *LinkedIn company pages and groups/discussion boards (general)*
- *Google Circles*

The first team is very much about connecting people in their knowledge needs. The second string is more generalised, with fewer personal connections, but is easier and cheaper.

In addition to these marketing offerings, client-facing KM can encompass the following, which would be 'first team' in marketing terms, but fairly costly for the firm:

- Portals with relevant information and extranets
- Sharing precedents and simple document assembly
- Sharing information professionals' time with clients (free research and library facilities)
- Secondments and mentoring

A lot of the first team client-facing KM is highly tailored and expensive, so it is important that the firm identifies its key clients and concentrates on those. A firm can identify its key clients by analysing the volume of work, its flow and profitability.

Why clients like client-facing KM

In-house legal teams often feel exposed in relation to current awareness; they can't afford the cost of the online subscription services that law firms buy in. It is one of those things that keeps clients up at night, so is a clear value-add for law firms, but success for your firm will depend on making it relevant, readable and making it stand out from your competition.

How client-facing KM helps your firm

Client-facing KM brings your existing clients closer to your firm and reinforces the firm's brand, encouraging personal connections and loyalty. It also helps to bring law firm staff and clients together at all levels, so that your firm is not reliant on one key relationship with one partner.

There follows a brief summary of areas of client-facing KM your firm may wish to consider using. This handbook isn't a marketing textbook so these are only brief and are primarily a few practical ideas and top tips for success.

Whichever your firm chooses to use, remember to re-use any developed knowledge as far as possible.[3]

Client-facing KM services for existing clients

Extranets

Extranets became popular with larger firms and their key clients for a while, but have recently suffered from the information overload problem. Simply put, a client doesn't want 12 different extranets with 12 passwords and log-ins with 12 lots of similar current awareness and nothing special, from all 12 firms on its panel. Extranets can be useful where they are personalised to that client, perhaps with plenty of precedents of minor legal documents, perhaps some form of document assembly, so in-house counsel can prepare some documents for themselves, but unless they are special, many clients will not use them.

Secondments

These are one of the most expensive forms of client-facing KM, but they provide an unparalleled opportunity for a law firm to build a closer relationship with that client. It is, of course, tempting to send the cheapest fee earner, but remember that the person that you send is your ambassador and will be given the opportunity to forge a brilliant relationship with this client. Do you want this to be a paralegal with little firm loyalty or could you afford to send that promising junior lawyer who wants to make a name for themselves within your firm? You won't want to lose them to the client or miss the opportunity to get as much business intelligence as possible; some juniors won't necessarily understand what your business needs to know and won't have many opportunities to network with the true decision makers.

KM Help

Some firms offer key clients help with their knowledge resources, such as help from their information team (as long as it isn't answering a legal question).

Many clients have out of date libraries and ad hoc paper-based collections. You could offer an audit, either as a value-add for key clients or as a paid-for service. You could offer a book-buying service, loose-leaf service or legal research training. Once you understand what your clients' headaches are, you can offer knowledge services to fit that gap.

Client-facing KM for marketing to existing and new clients

The first team

Seminars

These are an obvious suggestion for the first team. Use the suggestions for training in Chapter 7 to improve your firm's seminars and remember to have a purpose in mind before each seminar so that you ensure the right clients are invited and your lawyers have networking aims in mind beforehand, and follow-up targets afterwards. You can also invite certain key clients to your own internal training sessions.

Articles in external publications

Articles in external publications aren't face to face or personalised, but they are still a powerful tool. Here the important aspect to get right is the choice of publication.

Articles in professional journals may bring glory to your lawyers as experts in their fields, but they won't bring in customers. I personally fell foul of this early on in my consultancy career. I wrote lots of articles for KM-related journals and then found at my first pitch that the potential client had never even heard of the journal, let alone read my article!

Articles in your clients' trade press single your lawyers out as experts in their fields, so they are rightly cast as 'first team' by Maister. They also have multiple uses. They impress on initial reading, and then they can be handed out later at seminars to attendees, giving added authority to your speakers. They can then be sent to targeted clients who express an interest or who have a particular issue and, lastly, Maister suggests collecting them together and binding them as a book, to be kept at reception or sent out to clients, far more impressive than a brochure or leaflet.[4]

The second string

Newsletters and newsflashes

Many law firms produce monthly or quarterly newsletters, often because other law firms do. What keeps newsletters and newsflashes in the second string is most law firms' inability to go beyond detailing the nuts and bolts of what has recently happened or how the law has changed, and to include the 'how does it affect me?' and 'so what do I need to do now?' aspect, tailored to each client. A truly useful newsletter or newsflash will cut through the noise far better than general newsletters. Of course these types of articles take more thought than the usual general comments, but the extra effort will make your firm's newsletters stand out.

Although an element of cross-selling is valuable in a newsletter, it needs to be subtle, such as a summary of what else is available that month, or a link to a page summarising everything, otherwise it becomes off-putting.

It would be ideal if each partner could generate a personal email with articles which would be particularly interesting to individual clients, but this is also time-consuming and marketing departments tend to prefer standardised mailings that they can track more easily using specialist IT systems. Perhaps this is another way that smaller firms can in fact outshine larger firms, as partners can concentrate on individual clients more closely, know them more personally and tailor their content marketing more closely to the recipients.

Social media

Social media is a fairly new medium for many smaller law firms, but it provides an excellent opportunity to have personal conversations with your clients, although with the proliferation of services, many law firms are confused about where to focus their efforts. I would recommend law firms look at LinkedIn, publishing a blog and a couple of Twitter accounts; however if your market research suggests that your clients spend more time on Facebook, you should create business pages there as well. Of course when you start to use a new medium like social media, it brings with it new challenges. There is a Law Society Practice Note on Social Media[5] which is worth reading, giving some helpful reminders of how it can be easy to breach some of the fundamental principles, particularly the need to keep client information confidential.

LinkedIn for law firms

LinkedIn is a network for professionals. Individuals can have CVs/profiles and businesses can have their own pages with space for different products and services, jobs and special offers. A firm may have a business page and encourage its lawyers to have individual pages, but the most important factor, the one which takes this aspect of client-facing KM into the second string rather than the also rans, is judicious use of discussion boards and groups.

Discussion boards are a way for people to connect with each other and lawyers to hang out virtually with their clients and potential clients. It enables lawyers to showcase their expertise in a different way by posting useful links, sharing useful information and answering questions. As with writing journal articles, it is important when doing this for marketing purposes to join groups to which your clients belong, rather than other experts in your field.

If you are going to use LinkedIn extensively, it is worthwhile investigating the latest case law in relation to ownership of contacts, posting of CVs, etc. Currently individuals' lists of contacts can belong to the business rather than the individual if they are built up as a result of work at the business and individuals will need to be careful about soliciting for clients when they change roles. There isn't room in this handbook to cover this in detail, and any comments would probably be out of date as soon as the handbook is published, but be aware of potential issues and keep them under review.

Blogs

Blogs (a contraction of 'web logs') started as a type of online journal. Most law firms these days use them as a medium for broadcasting articles about their areas of expertise to existing and potential clients, and conversing with them through the comments section.

The important areas to concentrate on to make your blog work well as a marketing tool, is to choose the right platform (I like WordPress) with the right plug-ins to allow your readers to share your content with their followers, then fill it with quality content. I wouldn't worry too much about SEO (search engine optimisation) as your blog will be found by search engines if you have plenty of quality content, which will naturally be rich in the key words your audience are searching for.

If you find your blog isn't getting the readership you hoped for, check that you invite engagement, write about topics of interest to your clients and aren't being too 'sales-y'. Those reading blogs expect a more relaxed writing style than lawyers are used to, so blogging may take a little time to get used to.

There is lots of advice available online about successful blogging, if you are interested, but I'd recommend that you keep it simple to start with and build a following slowly, learning as you go.

Twitter for law firms

Twitter is one of the social media services of which I am a fan but many lawyers 'don't get' or are afraid of. It is a global phenomenon. With over 300m users, its business potential can no longer be ignored. It is no longer where star struck fans stalk celebs or narcissists tweet about their coffee habits,[6] but it is where you can find out the latest news from the Law Society of England and Wales, your favourite chambers, newspapers and maybe also your competitors and clients.

BOX 8.3   Top tips for successful tweeting

There is no magic recipe, but these tips may help.

1. Listening

- Study your audience, your competitors and those whose tweets you enjoy, but don't feel you have to read every tweet otherwise you will soon be overloaded.
- Listen especially to your critics. Third-party applications can email an alert to you when someone tweets about you or any keyword or URL you choose and Twitter Search will make sure you see if someone is talking about you or your firm.
- When you start tweeting, continue to listen and join in relevant discussions.
- Always answer questions directed to you.

---

2. Post a balanced number of tweets

- Recommendations as to a maximum vary, but personally I recommend around five per day. Your audience will be impressed by quality not quantity;
- Most professionals I know are more likely to un-follow if you tweet too much rather than too little, but do try to tweet at least one message each week.
- If you include a suitable hashtag (#) in your message, the right people will be able to search and find your tweets over the noise.

3. Provide value to your followers

- Don't write anything you wouldn't want to read by a client. Be thought-provoking, pithy, interesting and engaging.
- Twitter works best for conversations, not just as an RSS feed or for press releases.
- The best self-promotion is subtle and interesting.
- Promote other people and re-tweet interesting people more than you promote yourself.
- Share links with a discussion point or explanation as to why it is interesting.
- Minimise the 'noise'. You want to shrink the emotional distance between you and your clients, but they don't really want to hear that you are having coffee again.
- Keep private messages private and just send a public tweet when it is of interest to many of your followers.

4. Try not to use automatic direct messages

- These may save time but they do little to build relationships or help you to connect with your followers.

5. Make sure your website/blog is up to date

- There is no point engaging people if you point them to a site with broken links, poor contact information, out of date newsletters/articles or old news, or no information about your seminar and events programme.

Measuring the success of social media

There are plenty of measurements you could take to ascertain whether your social media efforts are giving adequate return on investment which you could keep on a simple spreadsheet. Have a look at Chapter 9 for more ideas. Another way to measure influence across social media platforms, is Klout.[7]

Klout scores measure influence on a scale of 1 to 100, with 100 being the most influential.

Klout uses data from your social networks and measures how you influence people by creating or sharing content that inspires actions such as likes, retweets, comments and more. The more engagement your posts receive, the more influential you are.

Klout uses this information to provide you a Klout Score that measures your overall influence in three ways:

1. how many people you influence (True Reach);
2. how much you influence them (Amplification); and
3. how influential they are (Network Score).

An average Klout score would be 20 and it is harder to go from 70–75 than it is to go from 15–20.

I wouldn't recommend a slavish use of Klout, but it is another way of keeping an eye on your level of influence on social media.

Recognition and reward structures

It is important to support the requirement to offer client-facing KM with the right recognition and reward structure in order to support fee earners who do this work. It isn't sufficient to purely reward new client wins, as it is often the work of many lawyers, through seminars, newsletters and other media which build up to the client win.

Recognition and reward structures are considered in Chapter 5, but it is important to consider client-facing KM in appraisals to emphasise its importance.

Summary: The least you need to know

- Client-facing KM is nothing new and encompasses all kinds of quality content marketing that firms have been engaged in for many years.
- Client-facing KM tends to be in the 'first team' of marketing as it helps clients in ways they really need help and brings them closer to your firm, building loyalty.
- Client-facing KM is often one of the more expensive forms of marketing, so should be used strategically.

ANNEX 8A: Draft RATER questionnaire for firm X's clients

Please mark the following statements on a scale of 1–5, where 1 is 'not at all true' and 5 is 'completely true', or n/a (not applicable).

1. X provides me with the service that I have been promised.
2. X's service is consistent and timely.
3. The staff at X have the skills and knowledge needed to deliver a good service to me.
4. I trust the staff at X.
5. I am happy with the legal documents that X draft for me.
6. I am comfortable meeting X staff at their offices.
7. X's website is useful. It contains the information that I need and answers the questions that I expect it to.
8. X handles my queries and feedback satisfactorily.
9. I have a good relationship with the staff that I meet.
10. The letters that I get from X are clear and easy to understand.
11. I receive the right amount of contact from X, neither too much nor too little.
12. If I have a complaint in relation to the legal work that X carries out for me it is dealt with satisfactorily.
13. If I have a complaint about any other aspect of the work that X carries out for me it is dealt with satisfactorily.
14. I believe that X understands my legal problem.
15. I believe that X genuinely cares about solving my legal problem.
16. I can talk to my solicitor when I want to.
17. I can communicate with my solicitor in the way that I want to (by telephone, letter, email, in person, etc.)
18. Staff at X are always willing and able to help me.
19. Please explain if there is any other way that X could improve the quality of its service to you.
20. Are you a business client or an individual?
21. Do you live in the local area?
22. How did you hear about X?

ANNEX 8B: Project plan

A coordinated campaign, making the most of one piece of 'knowledge'.

Task	People	Timescale and date completed
1. Identify a group of clients that your firm wishes to improve relationships with. *If you are not used to holding these events, why not start by holding an event for a group of your favourite clients to give you a positive start?*	Senior fee earners. Marketing team.	
2. Identify an issue that interests them. *Again, if this is your first event, why not start with a topic that you know well?*	All fee earners. Marketing team.	
3. Identify a journal that these clients read.	Fee earners. Marketing team.	
4. Speak to editors about potential articles and content that they are happy to use.	Marketing team.	
5. Write the article and speak to the editor about likely publication date. *Do you want to buy enough copies of the publication to give one to each attendee at the seminar?*	Fee earner.	
6. Organise a date for the client seminar. *This should be around 2–4 weeks after your articles are published.*	Support staff.	
7. Re-purpose your article for an in-house newsletter or e-zine or blog-post. *You must re-purpose the article to suit the audience and publication. If they are virtually the same, check with your primary publication what their policy is about republication. Usually they are happy as long as you include a phrase such as 'this article was originally published in . . .'*	Fee earners.	
8. Re-purpose your article for other external publications, such as Legal Week, EzineArticles or whichever your client group uses. *See above.*	Fee earners.	

9. Write a plan to ensure that the seminar is held around 2–4 weeks after your primary article appears in the external publication and your internal newsletter. *You want the details to be fresh in the minds of clients when your seminar invitation arrives and when you present at the seminar.* *Are you clear about those you wish to invite? Make sure you have a clean invitation list at an early stage in the process.*	Support staff.	
10. Publicise your articles and your seminar on your website, blog, Facebook page, LinkedIn business and personal page, Twitter feed, and any other channel that you use. *Your marketing team should be able to tell you what media your client group engage with, although there is no harm in including other free sources.* *When using social medial, aim to keep it 'real'. People who engage with social media get turned off by sales broadcasts. You can easily get the message across, but you need to be savvy. Fee earners writing the articles can talk about the good and bad sides of writing, how it fits with their working day, ask for advice and engage with their followers for ideas and angles, talk about new things they have learned and link out to other people's research as they research their article – those who like social media like people who publicise others more than themselves.*	Fee earners. Marketing team. Support staff.	
11. Invite your core group of potential attendees. Don't be disheartened if few clients reply straight away. Do send reminders and get fee earners to mention the seminar when they interact with the clients – people are busy. I often want to attend something, then I get caught up in work, time passes and suddenly it is next week – I'm still keen to go and free, but I appreciate a reminder. It isn't a hard sell.	Support staff.	
12. At your event, as well as the usual copies of slides, have the following readily available for attendees: copies of the external publication and in-house publication, sign-up postcards for your in-house marketing. Write a list of what you gave to everyone, review it after the event (what did people like, what did they not like?) and keep it for next time.	Support staff.	
13. At the end of your event, ask everyone who appeared interested to provide comments and recommendations for your website, LinkedIn pages, blog, etc.	Fee earners. Support staff	

14. After your event, put your slides on your website, blog, Facebook page, etc. and onto SlideShare and publicise all over again through all channels.	Fee earners. Support staff.	
15. After the event, think about what you have learned and use it in all future client-facing KM. *Add the legal technical information to your in-house knowledge collection for sharing. Would an internal training session benefit your fee earners? What did you learn about the process of running the project? Did you create a project plan, list of contents for attendee-pack? These can all be reused. Also, what did you learn about the topic from your interactions with the audience? There is probably another article or blog post in there. Get input from everyone involved. Your support staff will also have valuable feedback about what went well and what didn't, to make the next one run more smoothly.*	Everyone.	

Hopefully this way you will have squeezed every last drop of use out of one piece of created knowledge (your original research into the topic) and minimised fee earners' non-chargeable time, as a lot of these tasks can be undertaken by support staff, and maximised publicity.

ANNEX 8C: Interview with Mark Gould, Head of Knowledge Management at Addleshaw Goddard

If you had one piece of advice you would give to non-Magic Circle firms about client-facing KM, what would it be?

The most important thing is very simple: to know your client. Firms need to have open conversations with their clients about what they want to achieve and then help them to deliver it.

Regional firms may have an advantage here over larger firms. Operating within a tighter commercial community provides them with more opportunities to get closer to their clients and, being closer to them, to have more opportunities to learn about what those clients really want, what keeps them awake at night, and so be more confident that they can give them in their client-facing knowledge marketing, what they need, particularly in terms of training seminars.

In relation to training, the important thing is to challenge your clients to tell you what will really deliver value to them, not just CPD hours.

Once that is clear, the firm will need to decide how they will deliver that: who will be involved, what resources they will allocate to it, what recognition will be given to those who have been involved. They can then reuse the knowledge created in that seminar in a number of ways: articles, in-house training, etc.

Client-facing KM has historically been an after-thought for fee earners because of the reward structures in place at most firms that reward primarily for the chargeable time that is recorded. How important do you think reward and recognition structures are? Do you think firms are starting to turn away from rewarding purely chargeable hours?

Recognition is easier to get right than reward.

As regards reward, in smaller law firms the politics of bonus structures are especially sensitive. Many firms try to solve this problem by being opaque in the way that they reward their staff, but this is unhelpful over the long term.

Many firms are now turning to a mixed system, whereby a chargeable hours target is set as an initial hurdle for eligibility for a bonus, then a second hurdle is set of additional KM or business development hours and it is only after both hurdles are cleared that a bonus is payable. This has the benefit of being transparent and is easy to calculate, but the problem is that staff may only fulfil their non-chargeable target then stop knowledge sharing or helping with business development, or may offer poorer quality work.

The main difficulty with these methods is that only inputs are measured – not all the chargeable hours may be billable and not all the non-chargeable hours may have value to the firm. In an ideal world a firm would assign a value to the output, especially to business development and KM work, and reward staff on that basis, but I accept that that is a difficult thing to do.

Recognition schemes are an easier way to promote knowledge sharing and business development. The key to successful recognition scheme is the firm's leadership. They need to model the behaviours they expect from their staff in relation to knowledge-sharing and business development and to recognise those staff who exceed expectations. This doesn't have to be something as formal as an employee of the month award, and in some ways all staff should be behaving as clients would expect, but some public expression of gratitude, perhaps a public story highlighting how one staff member's hard work played an important part in the customer's experience or in a business development or knowledge-sharing project, works well.

How has the recent recession and threatened double dip recession affected client-facing KM offerings such as extranets and use of a firm's information services? Are they still an important part of the tender process or is price the most important thing now?

Both – prices have been driven down and clients are still expecting the value-added client-facing KM offerings.

Many larger business clients are using procurement professionals, who understand and favour price and service level indicators during the tender process, but there are also lawyers on the client's panel who are concerned about how they can make their relationship with their law firm 'go further' than purely the matter transaction.

But the real change seems to be that clients and lawyers are now increasingly able to have more honest discussions about the value-add items within their relationship. Clients understand that all these add-ons are not without cost to the law firm, and they are more open to discussions about levels of work received where these don't match up to the levels of free additional service they receive. It isn't as straightforward as covering the cost, but there is far more understanding on both sides that there needs to be a return on the firm's investment in the client.

Have you ever valued a particular aspect of client-facing KM and if so, did it offer a good return on investment (ROI)?

I haven't scored individual seminars or newsletters to look at their ROI, but I do look across a market sector or work stream at the amount of input needed for seminars or briefings and study the results from that and then feed that information back into future planning.

About 6 years ago the Client Development Centre (CDC) at Addleshaw Goddard set up a very unusual leadership programme (comprising coaching, mentoring and simulation-based courses) for in-house General Counsel (GCs), to help them achieve the recognition they deserve from their companies for the quality of their team's work and the value they delivered for the business. The cost and value of the CDC's work is clear to the GCs who benefit from it, and it is provided on the basis that the firm will see a corresponding benefit, for example by way of additional work. The client understands that they pay for the course indirectly. This approach works because it is a unique offering, but I doubt it could apply to other seminar programmes, as in that situation there is always the risk a client will simply attend the seminars of a rival who is not expecting a return instead.

Even if there is no direct return for a seminar, there is value to it. Hopefully they provide an excellent showcase of a firm's skills and provide an opportunity for lawyers to discuss issues with their clients and get to know them better. At the very least, the client will return to his/her office with branded products and next time he/she has a problem, will have a visual reminder to call us.

It is important that client-facing KM offers a good ROI. If it seems like it is not improving recognition or additional work in, then those arranging the seminars must ask themselves and their clients, why the topics they are covering are not 'hitting the spot'.

What do you think is the place of social media in client-facing KM? Many firms seem to be resistant to using these media, especially Twitter.

A lot of firms seem to be stuck in a traditional publishing model and see Twitter as just another broadcast channel. I've not seen many successful Twitter-feeds from commercial firms (as opposed to individual lawyers), primarily because they aren't engaging enough.

I'd liken the Twitter relationship as similar to the traditional golf day: a lawyer wouldn't stand in a corner and intermittently shout out interesting bits of case law or about how great their firm is; they'd engage the clients in conversation, then, if they sensed the client wanted to discuss potential work, they'd exchange business cards and speak privately at a later date. Law firms ought to treat Twitter in a similar way, engaging in general discussions, then switching to direct messages (DMs) and telephone discussions with those who wish to engage with them.

This is another area where a smaller regional firm probably has a head-start on Magic Circle firms, as they are usually closer to their clients and have already formed closer connections, so can more easily engage in conversations over social media, although, of course, it all depends upon who your clients are. If they are on Facebook, not Twitter, you will have to engage with them there.

How can firms avoid creating too much 'noise', causing their message to be lost?

In my experience, this problem mainly occurs with 'news-flash' type emails, where there is a significant case in the news and the firm prepares a review of it for their clients. The difficulty is that the client will probably receive many, maybe a dozen, such emails from all of the solicitors that they instruct and none or only a few of them will address their personal business issues (since they are written for a wide audience of clients) so they are all binned. If a law firm could identify key clients and write personalised reports on key cases highlighting how that case affects that client's business, they would stand out from the rest and provide a useful service to that client.

In relation to more traditional newsletters, one problem is that many marketing departments are very keen on e-newsletter systems because they make it easy for them to track who is opening the newsletters and to ascertain who is reading which articles, which, in theory, will help those creating the newsletter to create more valuable content. The difficulty with this is that strict adherence to the digital marketing rules can mean that there may be little cross over between the mailing lists for different newsletters and little cross-selling. It is important, therefore, to give clients opportunities to 'pull' different information, perhaps using RSS feeds or including information about different newsletters in emails to enable clients to sign up to different subscriptions or download ad hoc newsletters that interest them from different groups.

The future – what do you think are going to be the key areas of change for non-Magic Circle firms over the next five years?

It is always tempting for smaller firms to try to emulate other larger firms, taking on PSLs, building large KM databases, etc. I think it most important that smaller firms recognise that their size is an advantage and gives them an agility that Magic Circles lack. A firm which has less resource to achieve what it wants can still create something valuable and something more closely aligned to its needs. A partner who feels that there is a need for a new knowledge tool of some sort in their department could look at what can be done with the tools they already have or those available for free in the cloud (password protected). These can be adopted gradually whilst maintaining a conversation with the department about what is proving useful about the tool and adapting the process to suit the group. A smaller firm can test an idea then adapt or discard it as it needs to with a minimal cost. In a Magic Circle firm with offices across the world, there are massive change management issues with any new system of work. Smaller firms can avoid those problems with closer personal connections.

The increase in offerings of external knowledge-providers such as PLC and LNB also give the smaller firm a useful head-start. In many areas of work now, servicing clients has become about offering an incremental value-add on top of the PLC offering, which is as easy/difficult in a smaller firm as it is in a larger one.

The key in smaller firms as in larger ones is always to ask oneself 'What do we need to achieve as a business?' and designing a KM strategy around that. The answers to that question change over time, but that question remains fundamental. If a firm is training up its own lawyers from LPC and training contract onwards, does it need to offer them wider experiences through secondments, mentoring or good training? On the other hand, a firm that tends to recruit qualified junior staff from larger firms who are used to lots of precedents will have different needs. KM can fix a lot of problems in different ways, many of which are not expensive or out of the reach of smaller firms (KM certainly does not = IT), the key is to understand and focus on solving the problem, not buying into the latest fashion.

ANNEX 8D: Twitter – is it for the birds?

What is Twitter?

Twitter is a real-time, micro-blogging, social networking site that enables users to post 140 character micro-blog posts – or 'tweets' – which their followers choose to receive. The 140 characters include all punctuation and spaces. Twitter is multi-modal, enabling messages to be posted and viewed from a computer (via the Twitter site or a desktop gadget), a personal digital assistant (PDA) or a smart phone. Originally, tweets answered the question 'What are you doing?', but now answer the question 'What is interesting you at the moment?', or simply converse with followers. Twitter can support pictures (via TwitPic) and links. By default, tweets are public but senders can restrict delivery to their followers or send direct messages.

How can law firms use Twitter?

There are three main potential benefits to firms and individuals in using Twitter:

- listening and research;
- sharing information; and,
- networking, building relationships and communities.

Whether Twitter will work as part of a firm's marketing mix, will depend upon its brand, business objectives, employees and most importantly, its clients and potential clients.

Listening, information gathering and research

Twitter has excellent search facilities (Twitter Search and Trending Topics) which can enable a firm to gather real-time market intelligence and listen to what customers, competitors and others are saying about it – albeit this is a particular cross-section of views (Twitter users) rather than the whole market. Twitter gives critics a forum but firms need to be aware of what their critics are saying and why, to be able to fully understand and address those problems. Some businesses have found that customers are prepared to offer feedback about minor complaints or desired features over Twitter, which they would never have bothered to contact the firm about directly to discuss.

Firms can also listen to their competitors and leaders in the legal field, to find out more about influential lawyers and converse with them about current legal events and trends.

For example, a firm might be about to tender for work. It would probably be helpful to know what is concerning that potential client at the moment, what the market is saying about them and your firm, and what the firm's competitors are up to.

Similarly, if a partner is about to telephone a potential client to arrange a meeting, it is helpful to know a bit about who they are and what they are interested in at the moment in order to chat more easily. Twitter can help with this kind of research, although it must be handled carefully to avoid seeming like a stalker.

Alternatively, a new lawyer turned professional support lawyer who is confused by KM jargon could follow key figures in the KM arena and be spoon-fed all kinds of KM information, such as hot topics, recommended blog posts, details of webinars and so on.

As well as information about a particular market, Twitter can help individuals with business services, by tapping into the knowledge of the crowd for advice about, for example, recommended hotels, restaurants or training courses.

Sharing information of interest

Twitter can be used to communicate a range of information to a market. It can be used as an alternative RSS [really simple syndication] feed, alerting followers to a change in a firm's website or publicising a link to the firm's monthly client newsletter, or to send additional and specialist detailed information – perhaps from a key rising-star lawyer, showcasing their expertise. Its immediacy gives users the potential to be the first to forward useful information, such as key case or new legislation commentary, to a wide-reaching audience, especially those on the move. This positions a firm's brand to their clients and maintains awareness.

Relationship/community building

Although Twitter can be used as a broadcast medium, it is best used as a medium for conversation and relationship building. All lawyers want to be at the forefront of their clients' minds: the trusted adviser of choice. Twitter enables firms to build relationships, shrinking the emotional distance between them and their clients, potential clients and others. In a global market that is tough on costs, clients think twice about personal meetings and marketing events, which removes the traditional opportunities for lawyers to build relationships. Twitter has the potential to be one of the tools that builds this personal relationship.

It can also enable a firm to share its human side, giving them a peak behind the scenes at new offices, new projects or events; whatever is appropriate to its market. Twitter also enables firms to ask questions, float ideas and solicit feedback from their market.

On a more personal level, joining conversations about key topics can build lawyers' reputations as experts in their field and can act as a virtual water cooler for home-workers, or connecting staff to other attendees to conferences to help them make the most of the event and networking opportunities by identifying other attendees before-hand using the event's #hashtag and tracking what is said during the event.

Getting started

Getting started with Twitter is easy and free. There are only four fields to complete on the sign-up page. First, choose an account name. For a firm perhaps its domain name less the .com or .co.uk or another easily identifiable name; it is best for professional individuals to use their real names, so they are easy to find. Second, enter appropriate profile infor-mation so potential followers know whose the account is and what he/she will be tweeting about. Third, add a photo or logo, and then add links to a relevant website and/or blog.

It is probably a good idea to 'listen' for a while before posting a first message. Following people with similar interests and also individuals, who others recommend (perhaps on follow Friday '#ff').

One of the key advantages of Twitter is that newbies are not immediately exposed to a huge audience in a new medium: everyone can dip their toes first, then build a following slowly. If the conventions, symbols and strange terms are worrying, Twitter has a 'learn the lingo' section at the 'Twitter for Business 101' website (visit **http:// business.twitter.com**).

Be strategic

Like many Web 2.0 enterprise tools, there is always the risk of wasting time unless the strategic aims for Twitter use are clear:

- Who will be the twitterer?

  - a KM professional;
  - the firm;
  - the lawyers as individual ambassadors for the firm; or
  - all of these.

- What are the aims?

  - build expertise in a particular niche (legal or KM);
  - send out information clients will find useful as quickly as possible;
  - build personal relationships between lawyers and potential clients, to be their trusted adviser of choice; or,
  - drive more traffic to a website.

Choose a couple of key goals and use these to dictate the nature of the posts. Don't get sidetracked into the objective of 'getting more followers' or increasing numbers without taking quality into account. Twitter works best as a conversation enabler, not as a megaphone. What is needed are followers who help to achieve the goals already set.

Potential disadvantages

Set-up costs on Twitter are minimal, so why hasn't every firm already adopted it? There are a number of potential disadvantages. First, despite low set-up costs, firms can't adopt every innovation due to lack of staff time for implementation, so it is important to focus resources on the innovations that best suit a firm's market. Many see Twitter as a purely personal tool, aimed at techno-geeks and not yet 'enterprise ready', so overlook its potential. Second, there is always a risk to a firm's reputation. Some clients are anti-Twitter and anti-Enterprise 2.0 generally, they see it as an unnecessary overhead, or are concerned that their lawyers are billing them for tweeting time. Also, like blogging, if staff are given the autonomy to tweet as they see fit, there is always the risk they will say something inappropriate, spill confidential information or open the firm up to criticism or litigation. Finally, there is a concern that Twitter could be a massive time wasting activity for staff. The majority of the disadvantages are HR problems (not Twitter ones) so if HR solutions are in place, with published codes and culture, the majority of the disadvantages should disappear.

Twitter is a quick, easy and effective marketing tool. Whether it is worthwhile for a particular firm will depend upon its business focus and its clients.

Measuring success

Finally, there are a number of quantitative and qualitative measurements that could be used to measure the success or otherwise of tweeting.

In relation to quantitative measurements, concentrate on the qualitative measurements that are linked to a quality feed:

- the tally of questions answered;
- retweets of the firm's tweets;
- problems resolved, positive exchanges and conversations;
- whether people are un-following;
- the Klout score (see Box 8.4);
- traffic to a website from Twitter or track click-throughs from the links on tweets.

In relation to qualitative measurements, simply ask followers what they think. Some companies have found that the communities they have built are actually quite keen to give them feedback and help them to build better products and services.

Some tips for successful tweeting

It may be tempting to delegate this task to one of the youngest members of staff, but consider the purpose of the feed and the audience aimed for and choose the tweeter accordingly. If the aim is to build stronger relationships through conversation with a variety of clients and potential clients, then a PSL or lawyer will probably be the best person.

If the Twitter feed is simply a kind of RSS feed, an IT department can probably identify a suitable third-party tool. There are many tools that can coordinate updates to Facebook, LinkedIn and blogs.

Whoever is chosen needs to have an easy, engaging style, with a love of language and the ability to write short, pithy posts. It needs to be someone everyone trusts and they need to understand the firm's brand values and Twitter strategy, as they will have that brand in their hands. If Twitter proves to be worthwhile, make sure there is more than one 'twitterer' at the firm. People take holidays and quit and sometimes it is nice for the audience to have a bit of variety.

An ideal strategy will have a central identity for the firm with the firm's usual broadcast information, but also have departmental or topic experts who can engage more in conversations on their topic and include more engaging information. Personally I take more note of a tweet from an individual that they are getting ready for and are excited about an awards evening, than a general press release that a firm has been nominated for that award. A personal tweet rises above the 'noise' far better than the formulaic ones.

Once the twitterer(s) have been identified, the firm needs to ensure that the tweets promote the firm's brand. Twitter is a recipient-controlled model, which means that if a firm is not posting interesting messages, it is easy for them to 'un-follow'. Successful feeds can take different forms and it will depend upon the intended audience what style is adopted.

Endnotes

1 There is more information about reading on RATER surveys at Appendix 2.
2 Maister, D. (2003) *Managing the Professional Service Firm*, Simon & Schuster UK Ltd, pp. 121–31.
3 Ideas for this are at Annex 8B.
4 Maister, D. (2003), p. 126.
5 The Law Society of England and Wales 'Social Media' 20 December 2011 **www.lawsociety.org.uk/productsandservices/practicenotes/socialmedia/ 5049.article** (accessed 11 April 2012).
6 There is a detailed consideration of Twitter at Annex 8D.
7 **www.klout.com**.

Chapter 9

Measurement

This chapter covers the following:

- How law firm profitability is measured
- The value of measurement in KM
- The difficulties of measurement in KM and its unintended consequences
- How to use the balanced scorecard and other quantitative and qualitative measurements

---

Introduction

There are two truisms that sum up measurement of knowledge management activity:

'What is measured gets managed',

and

'You get what you measure'.

They are different sides of the same coin and reflect the fact that what is valued within a business is focused on and measured, but that this can have unexpected and negative results as well as positive ones.

It is also true that in professional services businesses, the benefits of knowledge management (KM) are usually intangible, or the way that KM affects tangibles can be complex, so that measurement is difficult. However, just because the value of KM can be difficult to measure, that doesn't mean that a firm shouldn't try.

There are probably two aspects to measurement in KM: measuring the value of a business as a whole, and measuring the value of individual knowledge systems or projects. This chapter will focus on the latter, enabling you to weigh the cost and overheads of a KM system or project against its benefits, so that you can make informed decisions as to how to develop those systems. If you want to learn more about valuing the knowledge within a business as a whole, there is additional reading suggested in Appendix 2.

This chapter won't make you an expert in the Skandia Navigator or fuzzy logic, but it will help you understand why you ought to try to measure the effectiveness of your knowledge systems, what you could measure and how, and where to start. Also, forearmed with details of the problems others have experienced, you can hopefully avoid these too.

Measuring law firm profitability and the productivity conundrum

Before you start measuring the value of some of your KM activities, you need a good grasp of how law firm profitability is measured and the productivity conundrum. Most readers probably have a good understanding of this, so this is just a summary, but there is further detail in Chapter 1 and further reading in Appendix 2.

Traditionally, lawyers charge their clients based upon the number of hours that they have worked on that client's matter. Whilst there are fixed billings and uplifts in some areas, this is the traditional model. Lawyers are set chargeable hours targets and their performance measures are based on the hours that they charge and bill and how much of this is realised.

Taking overheads off the total billings will give a figure for profit and dividing this profit figure by the number of equity partners, gives PPEP (profit per equity partner).

PPEP is immensely important to law firms and drives much of their business strategy. League tables are drawn up of firms' PPEP and law firms compete to improve their PPEP and their position in the tables. One cannot underestimate the importance of a firm's PPEP.

To understand one of the key difficulties in measuring the value of KM systems, one must first understand the productivity conundrum.

Traditionally law firms bill their clients in relation to how much chargeable time they have spent on a matter, rather than the value that they have added to their client's business. If drafting a contract takes four hours of a partner's time, for which she charges £200 per hour, the client is billed £800.

If, by using precedents prepared by experienced lawyers (taking perhaps three hours at £150 per hour) held on a new bespoke IT system (costing thousands of pounds) the partner is able to draft this contract in two hours, she bills £400. Thereafter she must either have more work to fill in the spare two hours or be unproductive.

Intuitively there are benefits to effective management of knowledge within a knowledge business such as a law firm, but viewed in this simplistic way it can be difficult to understand how those benefits fit with the traditional measurements of chargeable hours and PPEP.

To begin to understand where knowledge systems may help law firms, one must study a law firm's PPEP from a different angle. In *Managing the Professional Services Firm*,[1] David Maister separated out the business elements that contribute to PPEP, enabling firms to determine what factors drive profitability and hence improve a firm's health and hygiene factors.

PPEP = average realised rate x leverage x margin x utilisation

where

average realised rate = average hourly rate achieved by the firm or total billings/ number of hours billed
leverage = total number of fee earners divided by the number of equity partners
margin = profit of the firm
utilisation = total number of billable hours recorded divided by the number of fee earners[2]

Looking at PPEP in this way, a firm sees that while it can improve its profitability to a certain extent by increasing utilisation, this tactic has a ceiling: no matter how dedicated a firm's lawyers are, they will have to have a little time away from the office at some point. Even if they care little for their work-life balance, they will need to eat and sleep. Similarly, margin management (management of billing times, levels of support staff, space and equipment costs) can only be managed to a hygiene level, before it stops improving long-term profitability.

A firm can, however, continuously improve its long term profitability by improving its 'health factors', i.e. improving its leverage to the highest appropriate level for the category of work and developing value-added services which enable the firm to improve its hourly fee levels. It is here that KM can help law firms and is a good starting point for tangible ways to determine the value of a knowledge system.

The value of measuring

Valuing 'knowledge' and systems which improve how knowledge is shared and used within a complex business such as a law firm, is difficult. Some say it is impossible: knowledge is purely what happens internally when a person processes information and is constantly changing as that person's experiences inform the processing of new information. That may or may not be true and is an argument for a different book, but the pragmatic truth is that those who run law firms need to understand what return on investment they will get for spending on KM; those that run KM projects need to understand which of their projects are offering the best value for money and whether they should roll out that pilot across the firm or not; and lawyers (who would rather spend their precious time on chargeable matters) need to understand why there is a value in spending time on KM instead.

The productivity conundrum makes clear tangible proof of return on investment in sterling seem impossible, unless fixed price billing is used. Also, the benefits of KM are usually intangible, or affect tangibles in a complex way, so its measurement is difficult; however, 'Not everything that counts can be counted; not everything that can be counted, counts' (Einstein).

How to start with measuring results

When you start to measure some of your KM projects, perhaps to decide which give the highest return on investment, or to decide whether a pilot has been successful and ought to be rolled out across the firm, the first questions you will need to ask before determining how to measure are:

1. Why do you need this measurement?
2. What is the business benefit of knowing this answer?
3. What are you going to do with the results? What can you afford to change?
4. What can you afford to spend on measuring results?

Your answers to these questions will inform the nature of the measurements you undertake. There is no point in measurement for measurement's sake and in fact too many measurements can be counterproductive as they can create confusion, so take a balanced view of measurement, but take the minimum measurements needed to inform your decision making.

When you understand why you are measuring and how much you can afford to spend on measurement, then begin by looking at where you currently are. You must understand this first, in order to understand whether the change has improved KPIs or not. You must also measure in the same way before and after the change, for the results to be worthwhile.

You can measure the tangibles (effect on profitability, repeat business won, reduction in written time off, client satisfaction) more easily than the intangibles (what is the value of a well-run team meeting?), so tangibles are a great place to start, but that doesn't mean it isn't worth looking at the intangibles, especially if you get some unexpected results from 'you get what you measure' when measuring tangibles from people intentionally or unintentionally gaming the system (see p. 140).

BOX 9.1   Top tip

To the extent possible and productive, use measurement systems that are already in use within your organisation: presumably these measures exist because they relate to something important for the business, and this allows you to integrate your results within organisational reports and report to the executive board in a language and using figures they are familiar with.

Keep in mind the audience for your measurements and the purpose: are you measuring for those who allocate resources, for the users, for those working in KM, or for clients? What data will this particular audience need to see in order to be persuaded of a particular course of action? What would 'success' look like to them? If you are uncertain, ask them. Different stakeholders are convinced by different data and no matter how good you think your measurements are, if you don't convince your audience, your measurements have failed.

For example, your firm wishes to broaden its client base, perhaps becoming concerned that it is too reliant on a few large clients. There is a big emphasis on winning new clients, which means that it is involved in many more tenders and partners are under pressure to win more tenders. The KM department wishes to support this goal by developing a body of information about best practice for tenders and a collection of precedents or standard clauses that are often used and introduce a form of after action learning to accelerate improvements over the year. In this example, the firm could keep track of the process in a table like this.

Business goal	KM actions	Audience	Measure
• Improve PPEP by 20% over next 5 financial years • Improve % of tenders won by 20% over next 5 financial years • Increase chargeable time recorded by all fee earners by 10% over this financial year	• Develop 'tenders' area of intranet, including knowledge pack, precedents/ standard clauses, after action learning wiki (within 10 weeks) • Develop/improve thereafter (continuous)	Executive Board and Partnership	

The business goals should be SMART (specific, measurable, attainable, realistic, with a timescale) and you need to have an idea of:

- what success will look like;
- what you are going to do if your measurement goes in the direction you hope; and
- what you are going to do if it doesn't.

If you can't take action based on the measurement don't waste time and money on that aspect (i.e. if you can't afford to do anything about your old creaky client/customer relationship management (CRM) system at present, there is no point gathering data about the benefit of a new one). Focus your time and money measuring aspects that you can improve. You can always return to more difficult matters later (i.e. when profits pick up and a new CRM is possible if the return on investment allows). If you are unsure whether your measurement is actionable, ask yourself whether you want the measurement to go up, down or stay flat. If you don't know which way you want the measurement to go, or don't know what you will do if it goes up, down or stays flat, the measurement is not actionable and you need to think again.

How you measure the value of an existing system (a knowledge database or a system for delivering current awareness) or a new project (a new training and collaboration system) will differ greatly. All existing systems have costs attached, although these are more obvious in new systems than in old ones.

Then you need to decide on the practicalities:

- What measurements are you going to take and how are you going to take them?
- Who will collect the data?
- How, when and where will they collect it?

You need to describe it in sufficient detail to ensure consistency. Link your measurement to existing business measurements and key performance indicators (KPIs), but only if these give a real insight into the value of KM activity. Don't settle for a particular result just because the data is already there. It will end up being a waste of time.

Take a mix of quantitative and qualitative, leading and lagging measurements. You need a variety of measurement types to approximate the truth and even out any gaming. Informal discussions are just as important as formal soundings, so get to know what people really think by discussions with them. Find out what their drivers are and how you can really help them in their work. User surveys are extremely valuable for qualitative research, but can't be used too often because of user-fatigue.

BOX 9.2   Looking back and looking forward

Lagging indicators are measurements of things that happened in the past, such as financial results. These are often the easiest measures to develop and they give sound results about whether what you have been doing in the past has been working or not.

However, just as past performance is no guide to future performance on the stock market, your KM systems' past performance will not always be a great indicator of its future performance.

You will therefore need to also measure leading indicators as well. Leading indicators are those which refer to inputs, such as the cost of a new KM project (in time or spending on technology) and activity measurements, such as numbers of downloads of a precedent or regular contributors to a wiki.

For example, if you have an existing precedents system, you may want to keep an eye on whether it is fit for purpose, so you might want to measure the following:

- How often the tools are being used

    - Quantitative, leading – web stats, surveys, usage, number of docs available, number of new docs made available

- Ease of use

    - Quantitative, leading – load times

- Value placed upon them

    - Qualitative, leading – focus groups, surveys, consultation sessions

- Affect on firm's KPIs

    - (lagging) affect on business objectives (units charged, conversion, non-chargeable time recorded, leverage, PPEP)
    - (leading) level of new business won as a result of cross-selling

Once you have your data, remember that all measurements are not equal in value: 'non-chargeable time saved' is unlikely to be more important than quality, firm reputation or new business won.

You will also need to look at trends over time, not just snapshots, keeping in mind whether you have adapted your measurement system over time, to make sure you are still comparing apples with apples.

You need to understand what is truly important to the firm to ensure that you concentrate on the right aspects. You could measure hundreds of things about your intranet, but if you concentrate on quality and trust in its content, fee earners may forgive the fact that there are gaps in content.

Returning to our 'tenders' example earlier, the table could be completed as follows.

Business goal	KM actions	Audience	Measure
• Improve PPEP by 20% over next 5 financial years • Improve % of tenders won by 20% over next 5 financial years • Increase chargeable time recorded by all fee earners by 10% over this financial year	• Develop 'tenders' area of intranet, including knowledge pack, precedents/ standard clauses, after action learning wiki (within 10 weeks) • Develop/ improve thereafter (continuous)	Executive Board and Partnership	Quantitative, leading 1. Hits on 'tenders' intranet pages (monthly) 2. Downloads of precedents/ standard clauses (monthly) 3. Numbers of contributions to the AAL wiki (monthly) 4. Time spent by fee earners preparing tenders (using a specific time code) (monthly) 5. Time spent by fee earners in developing 'tenders' package (using a specific time code) (monthly) (KM staff time is considered a sunk cost) Quantitative, lagging 6. Number of tenders won and percentage (monthly) Qualitative, leading 1. Informal feedback discussions with user groups (monthly) 2. User group feedback survey and meeting to measure satisfaction with quality and ease of use (annually) 3. Post tender client feedback form (after each tender)

BOX 9.3   Reporting results – top tips

No matter how carefully you collate your data, you will need to communicate your results.

- Keep your audience in mind from the outset, when devising your measurement systems.
- Include the human face to the figures – few can listen to realms of figures and stay engaged, but a story or anecdote will have impact on your audience. Remember 'Salmon's Law' (Snowden) – people only believed that the Thames was no longer polluted once someone had caught a salmon. People need to witness the benefits of a measure (impressing clients, saving written off time, etc.) to believe the value, whatever the figures say.
- Know your audience when preparing your explanation of the results.
- Engage your audience's needs and wants – what the results mean for them.
- Give enough context so that people can understand the measure.
- Craft a communications strategy for your measures.
- Publicise your milestones, so people can see your achievements.
- Decide where and how to publicise the results. If you plan to release the results onto the intranet, who will see it? Do you want all the results available to everyone or do you want a more detailed version for the Executive Board and a slimmed down version for the firm as a whole?
- Use plenty of screenshots.

Unintended consequences and 'gaming'

The last topic this chapter covers is probably one of the most important and is part of 'you get what you measure'. Measurement systems can cause distortions in useful knowledge work and unexpected consequences, particularly where measurement systems are linked to performance either as a reward (part of the appraisal system) or a punishment (financial penalty to a department).

These distortions can be conscious or unconscious, as people change their behaviour to meet the targets set for them or the measurement systems applied to them.

There are numerous examples of unintended consequences to measurement systems in everyday life: teachers teaching to the test for SATs, not to benefit pupils' needs, but to improve their school's ranking; GPs refusing to book patients in for appointments at all, even when patients are happy to wait, so as not to breach government rules about patients waiting 48 hours before an appointment.

Lawyers and support staff in law firms are an intelligent group and, consciously or unconsciously, are likely to spot any weaknesses in your measurement systems and work out, consciously or subconsciously how to 'game' the results that affect them. Quantitative and leading measurements are particularly susceptible to gaming and so should always be balanced with qualitative measurements.

For example, if you measure numbers of submissions to a KM system and reward this, perhaps by noting it during annual appraisals, you may find a spike of submissions shortly before performance reviews. Of course this is not a problem if the quality is good, although it would be easier to manage if submissions were spread out throughout the year, but in truth, quality is unlikely to be good if 'box ticking' is the motivator. This can be done consciously, but is more likely to be that fee earners don't plan to give you substandard work, but they have been concentrating on other matters the rest of the year and give you the best they remember from the year. The firm gets what it measures, in that it emphasises fee earners meeting their financial targets each month, but emphasises other issues annually at appraisal time.

Similarly, if you measure page hits on particular intranet pages, those responsible for content (maybe PSLs or other fee earners) may start to manipulate content to increase viewing figures. Again, this is not a problem if the changes draw more people to view useful information, but if it doesn't, it is a waste of valuable time.

'Gaming' is difficult to avoid: people are almost always smarter than systems and will 'game' systems subconsciously, but you can approximate the true situation if you approach measurement from a number of different angles and use a mix of quantitative and qualitative, leading and lagging measures, and by being aware of the risks of gaming and keeping an eye out for unusual results or improvements in quantitative results which don't reflect an improvement in quality.

BOX 9.4   Ten measure design tests[3]

In relation to measuring the success or otherwise of KM systems, some of these tests will be more relevant than others, but all should be considered.

1.   The truth test – are we really measuring what we set out to measure?
2.   The focus test – are we only measuring what we set out to measure?
3.   The relevancy test – is it the right measure of the performance measure we want to track?
4.   The consistency test – will the data always be collected in the same way whoever measures it?
5.   The access test – is it easy to locate and capture the data needed to make the measurement?
6.   The clarity test – is any ambiguity possible in interpreting the results?
7.   The so-what test – can and will the data be acted upon?
8.   The timeliness test – can the data be accessed rapidly and frequently enough for action?

9. The cost test – is the measure worth the cost of measurement?
10. The gaming test – is the measure likely to encourage undesirable or inappropriate behaviour?

Updating your measurements

As you gain more experience in measuring your KM systems, you will need to update them. The firm's needs will change, it will grow, adapt to different clients, change its IT systems, etc. You will need to identify any goals that have multiple measurements and simplify them. You will need to replace measurements that are proved to be unhelpful, or those that have become too costly to justify. You will need to keep a delicate balance between continuing to stay the same (so you can identify trends over time, measuring apples against apples) and adapting to new circumstances and simplifying and focusing your measurements.

Measurement: the balanced scorecard

Whilst this chapter is primarily about measuring individual KM projects or systems, you may still be wondering about a wider, whole firm view of measurement. This book aims to be a practical guide, so details of the Skandia Navigator is beyond its scope,[4] but a review of the Balanced Scorecard is useful, as it has applications beyond whole firm measurement and strategy into individual department measurement as well.

The Balanced Scorecard was first proposed by Kaplan and Norton in 1992[5] and updated in 2000.[6] They understood that 'What you measure is what you get' and that traditional financial accounting measures, such as earnings per share and return on investment can give 'misleading signals' and negatively affect a business's ability to innovate and improve continuously.[7]

The Balanced Scorecard emphasises a simple but balanced perspective, using a handful of hard and soft measures and leading and lagging indicators. It is built around four key areas and asks four basic questions:

1. How do customers see us? (customer perspective)
2. What must we excel at? (internal perspective)
3. Can we continue to improve and create value? (innovation and learning perspective)
4. How do we look to shareholders? (financial perspective)

It aims to act like 'dials in a cockpit' so that managers can take in complex information from all four perspectives, at a glance, minimising information overload, and allowing managers to make sure that improvements in one area (say financial) are not at the expense of other areas (customer perspective or innovation/learning).

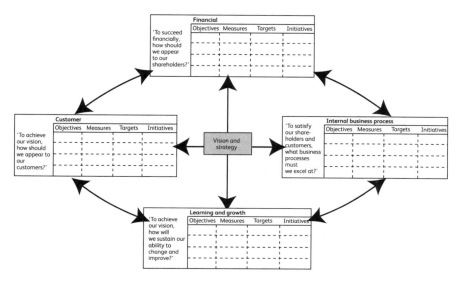

Figure 9.1　Measuring knowledge management sytems: the balanced scorecard

(Reproduced with permission of Harvard Business Publishing from Robert Kaplan and David Norton, 'Using the Balanced Scorecard as a strategic management system', *Harvard Business Review*, Jul/Aug 2007, vol. 85(7/8), p.153.)

While the Balanced Scorecard was designed for whole business strategy, individual KPI scorecards can be used for departments and teams where a strategic programme already exists at a higher level. With its emphasis on a balanced view, taking into account non-financial goals and measures, the balanced scorecard is ideal for KM departments in larger firms or for taking a 'KM view' of the whole business in smaller firms.

The balanced scorecard blends looking back and looking forward. It is fairly easy to measure what has happened in the past (outputs or lagging factors). This will tell you whether what you have been doing has been working or not, but it won't tell you what to do in the future. Leading indicators are input measures, such as the ongoing costs (of staff, of IT) and activity measures such as level of participation (web page views, amount of activity on a wiki, perceived utility of KM system as reported by users). Both leading and lagging factors can be quantitative or qualitative. There is a list of possible measures at Annex 9A.

The important point about all these measures is to use a spread of measurements to reach a more accurate result.

BOX 9.5   Outline of a plan for measurement

1. Define the business objectives of measurement and understand what success will look like.
2. Identify those being measured and the audience for the results – each stakeholder views KM and defines KM success differently.
3. Decide what data will be collected and how.
4. Analyse and communicate the measures.
5. Take action in relation to business objectives based on the results.
6. Review your combination of measures to ensure the right balance of quantitative and qualitative and adjust as your goals develop.
7. Keep under review unexpected consequences and 'gaming' the system of measurement.
8. Don't measure everything – focus on what's important.

Summary: the least you need to know

- For the most successful measurements, use a mix of quantitative and qualitative, leading and lagging measures.
- Focus on the purpose of the measurement and adapt it to suit the audience for the results.
- Keep your results under review and adapt your measurements accordingly.
- Act on your results.
- Be wary of gaming and unintended consequences, perhaps by looking at the 10 measure design tests.

ANNEX 9A: Potential ways of measuring KM systems

Quantitative:

1.   System user statistics.
2.   Hits on a web page.
3.   Load times of web pages.
4.   Usage of externally provided KM (i.e. by PLC, LNB, Justis, etc.).
5.   Uses of a precedent/the precedent database.
6.   Numbers of contributions to knowledge database.
7.   Numbers of queries raised and responded to.
8.   Time taken to respond to queries.
9.   Training events prepared/attended.
10. Length of time devoted to certain (perhaps non-chargeable) activities (e.g. preparing tenders or client seminars).
11. Non-chargeable time recorded.
12. Speed of document production.
13. Time to create new knowledge.
14. Number of repeat complaints.
15. Professional indemnity insurance claims.
16. Number of identified experts.
17. Number of people active in Communities of Practice (COPs).
18. Number of new employees.
19. Level of staff retention.
20. Retention of key staff.
21. Numbers of clients lost to leaving staff.
22. Number of knowledge debriefs.
23. Number of knowledge stories.
24. Invitations to speak at conferences/seminars, etc.
25. Number of publications in relevant literature.
26. Number of contacts with knowledge institutes.
27. KM budget availability.
28. Proportion of employees making new idea suggestions.
29. Time to develop new ideas.
30. Ratio of new ideas generated to new ideas implemented.
31. Percentage of sales earned with new knowledge.
32. Savings by knowledge re-use.
33. Reduction in cost of quality.
34. Information maintenance costs.
35. KM IT tool outage levels.
36. Level of leverage within a department.
37. Percentage profit from fixed fee work.
38. Utilisation level within a department.
39. Realisation levels within a department.
40. Change in ranking in Legal Directories.

Qualitative:

Could be measured by surveys (of fee earners, of support staff, of supervisors), focus groups, consultations, etc.

41. Ease of access.
42. Quality of document production (that is, fewer mistakes).
43. Ease of location of an expert.
44. User (both fee earner and support staff) satisfaction.
45. Confidence in the systems (success stories).
46. Quality of contributions to knowledge databases.
47. Sharing and use of best practices.
48. Ease of employing quality staff.
49. General employee satisfaction (both fee earner and support staff).
50. Tool availability.
51. Knowledge user complaints.
52. Knowledge user satisfaction.
53. Client satisfaction in quality of legal work.
54. Client satisfaction in supporting client-facing KM (portals, newsletters, seminars).

Endnotes

1   Maister, D. (2003) *Managing the Professional Service Firm*, Simon & Schuster UK Ltd.
2   Ibid, pp. 31–9.
3   Neely, A. et al (2002) *The Performance Prism. The Scorecard for Measuring and Managing Business Success*, Financial Times, Prentice Hall, via Chaffey, D. and Wood, S. (2005) *Business Information Management*, Pearson Education Ltd, p. 529.
4   Rumizen, R. (2002) *The Complete Idiot's Guide to Knowledge Management*, CWL Publishing Enterprises, Chapter 22.
5   Kaplan, R. and Norton, D. (1992) 'The balanced scorecard – measures that drive performance' *Harvard Business Review* January-February, pp. 71–9.
6   Kaplan, R. and Norton, D. (2001) 'Transforming the Balanced Scorecard from Performance Measurement to Strategic Management: Part 1' *Accounting Horizons* 15:1 March 2001, pp. 87–104.
7   Kaplan, R. and Norton, D. (1992) p. 71.

Chapter 10

The future

'The best way to predict the future is to invent it.' Alan Kay
'Look before, or you'll find yourself behind.' Benjamin Franklin
'We have inherited the past; we can create the future.' Unknown

There are many people who profess to be confident as to what the future of KM in law firms is. I'm not one of those people. These are particularly interesting times. As I write this last chapter in February 2012, the Legal Services Act (LSA) appears, so far, to have had a less significant effect (good or bad) on High Street Law than on Big Law. It is possible that the changes caused by the recession in 2008 pre-empted the predicted bloodbath, but it seems more likely that the effects the LSA will have on High Street Law have simply not yet started to be felt.

I fully expect to be proved wrong in relation to some of these ideas, but if there is one aspect which is entirely clear, it is that decision cycles will be shorter than firms are used to, and firms must keep their business and KM strategies under review and be quick and flexible in their responses to challenges from their markets. There is a real opportunity over the coming years for flexible dynamic firms, which respond to the changing market, to race ahead of their competitors to maintain and/or grow their firm's profitability and long-term health.

Why will law firms change? What demands are they facing?

Law firms, like all businesses in the twenty-first century, cannot continue to stay the same, continuing to do what they have always done.

Firms, especially non-Magic Circle firms, have already faced considerable pressure as a result of the 2008 recession and the public spending cuts to legal aid, and they face an uncertain future as the effects of the LSA are felt, in particular the Alternative Business Structures (ABSs).

In addition to these pressures specific to law firms, they also face the general problems faced by most businesses today: globalisation and the information age.

As discussed in Chapter 1 the information age has already brought a number of challenges to businesses such as law firms: information overload for staff and increasing levels of information freely available to potential clients. The sheer amount of information available causes difficulties for lawyers who have more information than ever to keep abreast of (changing laws and cases, regulations, industry and client news) some of which is from newly emerging sources, such as blogs and Twitter, and will need careful evaluation. The availability of this information to clients as well as lawyers also raises pressure on law firms to offer clients more than standard legal knowledge and documents. These no longer have the value they once did, but lawyers have valuable knowledge, skills and experience to offer and these challenges bring the opportunity to unbundle the simpler aspects of legal work, creating opportunities for new ways of working, particularly utilising non-solicitors, using new working practices, creating new products for lawyers to develop and sell, and creating new kinds of firms to meet different client needs. A traditional law firm which delivers quality, professional advice and personal service at an appropriate price needn't fear too much for the future, as some clients will always want to speak to a professional when things go wrong in their lives and will be willing to pay a premium for the personal attention of an expert, but those whose advice and customer service is poor, or who are confused about their place within the market and business strategy, will suffer.

Another of the other major changes is in working environments and work patterns. Apart from an increased need to be available to clients 24/7 via mobile devices, improvements in technology which support mobile working will enable lawyers to work at home or when out of the office seeing clients, freeing them to work more flexibly, but also putting pressure on them to work longer hours and to be more immediately responsive to queries. These mobile technologies will also put pressure on IT support services, whether in-house at firms or outsourced, as demand to support these new technologies increases, in particular the need to manage security, which is always a concern for lawyers.

How will law firms respond in the field of KM to these demands?

Successful law firms will respond to these pressures on multiple fronts: by adapting their business structures, through changes in management of their people, by improving their business processes and lastly, in relation to their IT.

1. Business structures

The pressures on law firms are likely to cause a proliferation of different business structures: intra-professional referrals, mergers, acquisitions, conversions to ABS, demergers. How are these different relationships likely to affect those working in KM in law firms?

Firstly, changes to business structures cause particular challenges to those working in KM. As one Head of Information said to me recently 'No matter which external providers you use, you can guarantee the firm that you merge with will have the others', so there is usually a lot of investigating, streamlining and reorganising to do. Similarly there will often be two IT systems supporting information management and search to reconcile.

Secondly, re-engineering of business structures causes change management issues. Staff worry about redundancies, changes to work practices and are unsettled by general upheaval. This is the same whether a firm is changing its structure and reporting lines, outsourcing its back office support services or managing a merger.

KM, information systems (IS) and IT staff often find themselves at the sharp-end of this fall out, trying to manage cultural changes with little or no training. A firm considering a change to its business structure would do well to invest in training some of its KM staff as change agents, and if you work in KM at a law firm, you may want to think about investing some time in understanding change management issues better.

Lastly, as smaller firms band together in formal mergers, or less formally to share costs of KM, IS and IT, there are exciting opportunities for all staff to learn from each other and review their work practices and experiment in working in different, more flexible ways.

2. Processes

(a) Increased demand for KM within all kinds of law firms

Old fashioned KM, where businesses bought expensive KM IT systems, then tried to extract every last ounce of 'knowledge' from its workers, turn that knowledge into lengthy, wordy documents and then put it into those databases, is dying, but KM as an activity which improves those business processes which involve 'knowledge' in some way, those which create, harvest, analyse, store, leverage, retrieve and retire knowledge in order to further that business's goals, has never been healthier.

As globalisation, increased competition and information overload place demands on law firms, they will need KM strategies more than ever before. Firms won't need more graveyard databases; they will need to understand and implement intelligent, streamlined workflows and work practices, better knowledge sharing and improved delegation, smoothing of the peaks and troughs of practice and to embed themselves in their clients' minds as trusted sources of knowledge.

One of the blocks to much KM activity has been the productivity conundrum, but increasing moves towards value-based billing and fixed fees will accelerate the demand for KM, to maximise efficiencies and hence profits.

(b) Right-sourcing

Over the past few years, there has been an increase in the amount of work outsourced in all sectors. Many law firms in particular have outsourced secretarial services, IT, HR, library services, document assembly, knowledge banks, precedents and current awareness. Some of this work has been sent off-shore and emerging economies are looking to increase their market share of quality work, such as legal work, in addition to the support services they already offer.

Over the coming years, larger firms will review outsourced and off-shored activities and analyse which have truly saved cost over the short and long term without affecting value and customer experience, and which have not. Smaller firms have the opportunity to see what larger firms do and analyse which work is brought back into the business, if any. There are many aspects of IS and KM which can be comfortably outsourced, but there will be some aspects that law firms recognise are part of their unique offering to their clients and ought to remain or return in-house.

Larger firms will more regularly in-source work, where they pass most tasks to their own in-house teams who are just as able, but work outside London where overheads are lower, to meet the pressure on costs, particularly from business clients. Clients are also likely to drive even more co-operation between panel firms.

Traditionally smaller firms have always outsourced some of their support functions. IT, payroll and HR are common outsourced services. They are likely to begin to experiment with informal groupings, sharing more sophisticated support services, but hopefully having the opportunity to learn the lessons of the larger, cutting-edge firms and avoid any outsourced work which saves cost but which affects the value within their business, to their customers and in their brand.

In particular, as externally held precedents become more common, all law firms will need to understand what knowledge is proprietary within their firm and what is generally known and understood. Before a decision on externally held precedents can be made, firms will need to understand pricing, licensing, terms and conditions, access and ownership, information and data security and how to manage the requirements of the Solicitors Regulation Authority.

(c) Measurement and strategic focus of KM activities

As overheads are squeezed by firms responding to increased competition by driving price down, KM activities are likely to come under greater scrutiny, but this needn't be a negative force. If firms are prepared to make intelligent use of measurement systems (see Chapter 9), they can focus their KM spend on matters which give them the greatest return.

Measurement was a popular topic within the profession, particularly amongst Magic Circle firms, in the late 1990s, but fell out of favour as the difficulty of the task became apparent and the benefits did not seem to justify the costs of complex systems of measurement. Much has been learned since then about measurement systems and avoiding 'gaming' and increased pressure for efficiency is likely to make measurement a popular topic once again.

Smaller flexible firms have a clear opportunity here, as they will be more easily able to respond to their metrics and adapt their business processes, than larger firms.

3. People

(a) What will the KM teams of the future look like?

The KM teams of the future will be noticeably different at different firms. Firms can no longer afford any spare capacity or underutilised staff. The KM team in each firm will depend on the business case at each particular firm, on that firm's place within its market, its differentiators and its business strategy.

Larger firms may outsource their library services and use some of the PSL type services offered by large subscription businesses, but there will remain a need for Knowledge Lawyers or PSLs to work on a firm's true differentiating value-add knowledge work, to facilitate the smooth sharing of knowledge between lawyers and to take an overview of work practices to produce an ever-adapting and improving best practice. KM teams are likely to remain embedded within their departments (the most common work practice at present), but they are likely to become more involved in strategy to ensure that their time is spent on valuable services which justify their salaries.

Smaller firms, challenged by new demands in their market, will investigate the value of KM strategies and more will buy in KM expertise, as they already buy in expertise from IT specialists, outsourced back office functions, marketing and help with compliance.

4. Technology

(a) Intelligent use of IT to connect people

For many years, businesses have looked for a single IT application which would be a true differentiator and solve all their business's knowledge-related problems. After much had been spent on databases, most firms realised that, beyond a certain level, the quality of the content of these wasn't sufficiently high, maintenance costs were significant, and usage was low. PSLs often found that not only were they spending time creating and/or editing the content on these databases, they were also duplicating this work, answering fee earners' questions, as fee earners preferred to talk to a trusted source rather than use the database.

Law firms are now likely to give up on the idea that they are looking for a single application to solve their business practice problems, and finally give up on those graveyard knowledge databases. I'm not against IT systems. They support the sharing of explicit knowledge (precedents, workflows, checklists, forms, contact information) brilliantly, but law firms need to understand the limitations of IT solutions and to understand that successful systems require a combination of technology, process and people. There is much that lawyers know that cannot be captured or transmitted in a written format. Now is the time that law firms will begin to realise the value of IT solutions which connect people, either by enabling them to speak to each other (such as corporate White Pages or Skype) or by facilitating written communication (such as instant messaging, discussion boards and blogs).

It is also likely that firms will learn from the mistakes of the past and embrace the need to give users the opportunity and responsibility for input to design, rather than rely as much on IT departments/providers. It has always been a waste of time trying to turn those round-peg lawyers into square pegs to fit into that IT-shaped square hole. It is far more efficient to make the IT fit the user, not the other way around.

(b) IT offers competitive advantage to smaller firms

As more IT businesses follow the 'freemium' business model, offering free services to smaller users and only charging larger users, smaller law firms have an opportunity to steal a march on their larger competition. Smaller firms have the opportunity to use IT more cheaply than larger firms and have the opportunity to adapt more quickly to changes, to be nimble, to try out new ideas and use them if they work or discard them if they don't. If they realise this, they will be able to grow new exciting businesses.

(c) Social media goes mainstream

At present, there is a lot of talk and activity around social media. There is a lot of enthusiasm for it amongst some business sectors and some business professions for marketing purposes, and a lot of concern about it amongst lawyers. There are law firms which have blogs, are on Twitter and a few which are on Facebook, but at present, very few 'do' social media well.

Lawyers are natural communicators, but they are also naturally conservatives. Their work often requires them to analyse the potential problems in new technologies and try to ameliorate them, or to pick up the pieces after things have already gone wrong. However, as their clients spend more time on social media, lawyers will realise that it is not a passing fad or a time waster, and see that they really need to get a grasp of the

152

technology and make it work for them and their clients. The coming generations of lawyers will be digital natives, who have lived their lives through social media and will not see the point of email, which will seem as outdated as fax machines do now. Coming to social media a little later than other business sectors needn't be a negative thing for the legal sector. Lawyers can learn from other business's experiences, avoid some of the problems they have experienced and bypass their learning curve, focusing their efforts on those media which have the greatest value for their firms, their lawyers and their customers.

Social media is not solely about marketing. It is also an excellent media for learning, connecting with like-minded professionals, forming relationships with complementary professionals and even job hunting.

There are likely to be a few casualties, as the profession gets used to a new means of communicating. There will be a gradual understanding of appropriate rules and responsibilities, and possibly a few casualties of the professional rules and a few mistakes made. Already there have been concerns about responses to questions over social media being taken as formal legal advice, but the profession's biggest problem is likely to be a surfeit of poor quality, dull broadcasting and a lack of good quality conversation and engagement, rather than too much sharing.

Lastly, there is one prediction which I wish I could make, but I can't: more intelligent use of reward systems. It will be some time before law firms are brave enough to move away from rewarding staff based purely (whether explicit in their targets or not) on the chargeable hour and billings. Perhaps as non-lawyers become more involved in running law firms, they will bring a fresh, pragmatic approach, with some new ideas, and similarly, as value-based billings and fixed fee work becomes more prevalent, there will be an opportunity to move the focus gradually away from the chargeable hour, but I doubt that this will be in the near future.

What I do envisage, is that those working in knowledge services within law firms will become more imaginative and effective in their use of recognition systems, for the benefit of the whole firm.

Summary

There is a bright future for flexible and dynamic law firms. It certainly won't look like the past, but those who rise to the challenge of increased competition due to the LSA, ABS and a changing landscape due to cuts to legal aid, as well as globalisation and the information age, who are innovative and open-minded about unbundled services and fresh approaches to work processes, have a unique opportunity to create worthwhile businesses which add value to society for the future.

In the future, KM techniques and strategies will form a golden thread running through all aspects of law firms, enabling them to manage their services better in order to further their business objectives, to secure them for the future.

ANNEX 10A: Managing change following a merger – the KM department

Times of merger can be difficult for information services and knowledge workers as well as other staff. One could write a textbook on this topic alone. There are different cultures to merge to form a new culture, different IT systems to cope with, different ways of working and many expert professionals on both sides with their own views about what the business ought to be doing.

I spoke to a Head of Knowledge Services at one regional firm[1] which had undertaken a merger recently and discussed the challenges mergers bring to knowledge-sharing cultures and systems at both firms. This particular merger involved one firm with a well-established knowledge-sharing culture and one firm that, whilst well resourced with a library and online services, was new to this concept. The challenge was how to develop a way of working that kept everyone engaged and collaborating and promoted an appreciation of the value of know-how.

We discussed some of the ways that that firm had tried to manage those problems, avoid too much disruption to services and grow a new joint knowledge-sharing culture at the merged firm. Neither of us pretends to have all the answers, but stories from the frontline are usually helpful.

If there was one key factor which you think helped to make your firm's merger a success in relation to knowledge-sharing, what would you say that was?

Communication. Good communication supports all the other success factors.

Staff can't always influence decisions. Sometimes there simply isn't the budget to give them the knowledge systems and support that they need, but if they are kept appraised of the options under consideration and the reasons behind decisions, then they are usually more understanding and accept the outcome or think around the problem together.

Good communication also means that staff are prepared for any changes, so the changes go more smoothly.

And the other factors which have helped?

The other factors would be strong leadership and trust.

I would also accept that we were fortunate in the timing of our merger and with our merger partner. The recession meant that some of our fee earners had capacity to help with work around the merger. This meant that everyone's time was well utilised and there was no need for any redundancies at either firm.

Our partner firm was also very understanding about the changes that they needed to undergo. Having had little in the way of KM systems before the merger, they were quite pleased with the suggestions we made.

If you were to advise another Head of Knowledge Services facing a merger, what advice would you give them?

It is important to stay aware of the things that are unsaid. There is bound to be a lot of office politics and power-play. You don't need to join in the politicking but you will need to be aware of what is happening, so that you can be sensitive to how staff are feeling.

Lastly, merger is an ongoing process. Just as building a knowledge-sharing culture is never a 'finished' project, so a merger is a long-term project. Just because the initial projects have been completed, doesn't mean that your role in building a collaborative knowledge-sharing culture is finished.

Knowledge-sharing requires trust between the parties and that is built slowly between individuals.

Endnotes

1   The contributor decided to remain anonymous in order to share his/her experiences more freely.

Glossary

After action learning (AAL)	Post-transactional reviews and matter debriefings undertaken to learn the lessons of each matter. These can take the form of meetings, forms on file closure etc.
Alternative business structures (ABSs)	The means by which non-lawyers can now, following the Legal Services Act 2007, own law firms.
Artefacts	The visible aspects of an organisation's culture: office furniture, how people dress, an organisation's logo, how offices and meeting rooms are set out.
Average realized rate	The average hourly rate achieved by the firm, calculated by dividing total billings by the number of hours billed.
Balanced scorecard	A performance measurement approach that links an organisation's strategy to five key measures: financial, competitors, customers, learning and internal business processes.
Benchmarking	Learning from the best to improve performance.
Best practice	Practices which have been outstanding in their situations.
Big KM	Enterprise-wide, top-down, structured KM.
Blog	Contraction of 'web log'. A personal journal published on the World Wide Web consisting of discrete entries ('posts') typically displayed in reverse chronological order, usually the work of a single individual, occasionally of a small group, often themed on a single subject.
Case management system	Usually used in relation to software. A system which standardises workflows and incorporates some precedents in order to leverage knowledge and manage the life cycle of a matter more effectively.
Client/Customer Relationship Management (CRM)	An approach to building and sustaining long-standing relationships with customers.

Client-facing KM	Aspects of knowledge management which are used for marketing purposes and/or value-added services, which face the firm's clients.
Communities of practice (COPs)	Groups of people who share a concern, a set of problems or a passion about a topic. They interact with each other on an ongoing basis to deepen their understanding of the topic. Whereas teams are created by management for a specific purpose, COPs are volunteers with fluctuating goals.
CRM systems	Systems, often technological, which support the long-term management of client relations.
Culture/Organisational culture	The way we do things around here. The values, beliefs and assumptions held by the people in an organisation
Current awareness	The updating of law firm staff, usually fee earners, with the latest legal and market information.
Customer relationship management (CRM)	Usually refers to software which manages a company's interactions with customers, clients and sales prospects, organising, automating and synchronising business processes.
Data	Discrete objective facts about events.
Delicious	A social bookmarking web service. Its community of users can create, store, share and use bookmarks of web pages. Users tag their bookmarked web pages with non-hierarchical, freely chosen labels (a kind of 'folksonomy').
Digg	A social news website, where the community of users can recommend content for sharing under various categories.
DIK(W) pyramid	A model for representing purported structural and/or functional relationships between data, information, knowledge (and wisdom).
Document assembly	Systems designed to take variable information from a user and generate completed or nearly completed legal documents. Variables may be words, short phrases, data, names of parties to a contract, the payment amounts, completion dates, etc. Generally menu-driven question and answer systems that guide the user through the document assembly.
Document management system (DMS)	Usually refers to software which provides a means to ensure that all documents are categorised in a consistent and logical fashion for easy retrieval at a later date, for re-use to leverage existing knowledge at an organisation.

e-Learning	Learning that is provided using an online medium, including You Tube video; online electronic support, virtual chat, quizzes and formal education programmes.
Explicit knowledge	Things we know that are easy to write down and share with others.
Extranet	An extranet is perhaps between intranet and internet. It is an intranet which uses internet protocols and public communications systems to work with selected external users, usually limiting access via a password and username.
Folksonomy	A taxonomy that is not imposed by an organisation, but is created by users.
Ground truth	The truth as it happens on the ground, rather than from the heights of academic study or generalisation.
Heuristics	Simple efficient rules, which may be innate or learned, which help people make decisions, but which sometimes lead to systematic errors. They include rules of thumb, intuitive judgements and common sense. Mostly, they are unarticulated.
Information	Data which sends a message; data which makes a difference.
Information management	The collection, management and distribution of information from one or more sources across an organisation.
Information systems	The means by which organisations and people gather, process, store, use and disseminate information, often through information technologies.
Internet	The global network of individual networks that are interconnected through the TCP/IP protocol for communication.
Intranet	Intranets use the same TCP/IP protocol, but they are controlled internally, private to the organisation and its employees and serve the business needs of the organisation.
Key performance indicator (KPI)	A performance measurement used by an organisation to evaluate its success or otherwise against its goals.
Knowledge	Information in context which produces an actionable understanding.
Knowledge café, Gurteen	A means of bringing a group of people together to have an open, creative conversation on a topic of mutual interest to surface their collective knowledge, to share ideas and insights and to gain a deeper understanding of the subject and the issues involved.

Knowledge cycle	Knowledge creation and construction, knowledge articulation, knowledge repository updating, knowledge access, knowledge use and knowledge revision and destruction.
Knowledge fair	A non-structured conference or fair, where those with expertise in an organisation share that expertise with the rest of the organisation.
Knowledge management (KM)	How an organisation identifies, organises, shares, captures and leverages knowledge to further its strategic goals.
Knowledge map	A process for identifying knowledge and skills within an organisation.
Knowledge spiral	A model proposed by Ikujiro Nonaka to represent how people share tacit and explicit knowledge to further a project goal within a business. Knowledge is consolidated and shared through four quadrants: socialisation (tacit to tacit), externalisation (tacit to explicit), combination (explicit to explicit) and internalisation (explicit to tacit).
Lagging indicator	A measurement which confirms what has happened in the past.
Leading indicator	A predictive measurement.
Lean management	A business methodology aiming to maximise customer value while minimising waste. A lean organisation understands customer value and focuses its key processes to continuously increase it.
Leverage	The proportion of non-partners to partners.
LexisNexisButterworths (LNB) and Practical Law Company (PLC)	Organisations which provide legal content, analysis and know-how for their subscribers.
Little KM	The quiet application of KM methods to solve business problems. Also known as stealth KM.
Margin	Profitability as a percentage and is calculated by dividing the profit of a team by the fees charged. The profit is its revenues less the direct and indirect expenses related to it.
Myers-Briggs type indicators	Myers-Briggs is a test to categorise people according to the way that they take in information, deal with people and make decisions.
Paradigms	Basic assumptions, theoretical frameworks.
Personal digital assistant (PDA)	A handheld device used to manage an individual's tasks. PDAs have combined diary, addresses, task lists, fax, telephone, web browser, etc., depending upon technology available at the time of design.

Personal knowledge management (PKM)	Where each individual is given the responsibility and the tools and training to manage their own knowledge needs throughout the knowledge cycle.
Portal	A web page that is the main entry into an intranet or the internet.
Porter's five forces	A framework for business strategy development, created by Michael E. Porter of Harvard Business School. This provides a framework for analysis of the attractiveness of a market through the study of five key attributes: the threat of substitute products; the threat of established rivals; the threat of new entrants; the bargaining power of suppliers; and the bargaining power of customers. It can be used to make a qualitative evaluation of a firm's current strategic position and/or a proposed change to position.
Porter's generic strategies	Three general strategic approaches which can be applied to products or services in all industries, and to organisations of all sizes: 'Cost Leadership' (no frills); 'Differentiation' (creating uniquely desirable products and services); and 'Focus' (offering a specialised service in a niche market).
Post qualification experience (PQE)	The number of years or half-years that a solicitor or legal executive has been formally qualified. For example, a solicitor must be at least 'three years PQE' and have undertaken a suitable management course in order to supervise a law firm's office, whatever their age and ability.
Profit per equity partner (PPEP)	PPEP=average realised rate x leverage x margin x utilisation
Practice management system (PMS)	Usually referring to software which is designed to manage a law firm's case and client records, billing and bookkeeping, schedules and appointments, deadlines, computer files and to facilitate any compliance requirements such as with document retention policies, courts' electronic filing systems and Solicitors' Accounts Rules.
Precedent	A template, a reusable standard legal document, used to leverage existing knowledge about that legal document.
Professional support lawyer (PSL)	An experienced fee earner, usually a solicitor of more than 5 years PQE, whose role is to manage the knowledge of their team/department throughout the knowledge cycle. They usually do not have chargeable time targets, but may charge for time spent on specific matters.

Quality management	A business methodology to improve the consistency of an organisation's product or service, through four main components: quality planning, quality control, quality assurance and quality improvement.
Sensemaking	The process by which people give meaning to experience.
Silos	Groups or departments which seldom share knowledge outside their group and seldom take into account how their work affects other groups.
Six sigma	A business methodology which seeks to improve the quality of process outputs by identifying and removing the causes of defects (errors) and minimising variability in manufacturing and business processes. It uses a set of quality management methods, including statistical methods, and creates a special infrastructure of people within the organisation ('Black Belts', 'Green Belts', etc.) who are experts in these methods. Each Six Sigma project carried out within an organisation follows a defined sequence of steps and has quantified financial targets (cost reduction and/or profit increase).
Social media	Web-based and mobile technologies to facilitate interactive dialogue and user-generated content, for example, blogs and wikis.
Social network analysis (SNA)	The mapping and measuring of relationships and flows between people, groups, organisations, computers, URLs, and other connected information/knowledge entities.
Storytelling	The telling of stories in order to help people retain information and lessons better.
Structured query language (SQL) database	SQL (pronounced 'sequel') is a programming language used for managing data in relational database management systems.
Tacit knowledge	Subjective insights. Knowledge that we don't necessarily know that we know.
Talk rooms	Common in Japanese industries. A room where employees meet, drink tea and discuss their work, exchanging valuable tacit knowledge.
Taxonomy	A classification system. An imposed hierarchical structure which makes a body of knowledge more manageable, by organising content into groupings within a framework.
Tesco law	See 'alternative business structures' (ABS) above.

Utilisation	The average billable hours recorded by the fee earners in a team or department (i.e. total billable hours for the team divided by the number of fee earners).
Web 1.0	Standard static websites, broadcasting information one-way to viewers.
Web 2.0	Interactive websites, such as blogs and wikis, where users can have conversations with authors/publishers.
Web 3.0	The semantic web, where content is tagged to help users find, share and combine content, to minimise noise.
Wiki	A website where users can add, modify, or delete its content. 'Wiki' is a Hawaiian word meaning 'fast' or 'quick'.
Wisdom	Knowledge with added insight.
Workflow	Diagram of streamlined work processes.

Appendix 2
Further resources

This is an ad hoc, purely personal collection of resources that may be of interest to you. I don't pretend to have created a comprehensive list.

Books

Chaffey, D. and Wood, S. (2008) *Business Information Management*, Pearson Education Ltd.

Collison, C. and Parcell, G. (2001) *Learning to Fly*, Capstone.

Dalkir, K. (2005) *Knowledge Management in Theory and Practice*, Butterworth-Heinemann.

Davenport, T. and Prusak, L. (2000) *Working Knowledge*, Harvard Business School Press.

Empson, L. (2007) *Managing the Modern Law Firm: New Challenges, New Perspectives*, Oxford University Press.

Hislop, D. (2005) *Knowledge Management in Organizations*, Oxford University Press.

Kelleher, D. and Levene, S. (2001) *Knowledge Management: A Guide to Good Practice*, BSI.

Leonard-Barton, D. (1998) *Wellsprings of Knowledge*, HBSP.

Maister, D. (2003) *Managing the Professional Services Firm*, Simon & Schuster UK Ltd.

Mekhilef, M., Olesen, A.J. and Kelleher, D. (2003) *European Guide to Good Practice in Knowledge Management* (see **www.scribd.com/doc/42700345**).

Neely, A. et al (2002) *The Performance Prism. The Scorecard for Measuring and Managing Business Success*, Financial Times, Prentice Hall.

Newell et al (2002) *Managing Knowledge Work*, Palgrave.

Nonaka, I. and Takeuchi, N. (1995) *The Knowledge Creating Company*, Oxford University Press.

O'Dell, C. and Hubert, C. (2011) *The New Edge in Knowledge: How Knowledge Management Is Changing the Way We Do Business*, Wiley.

Parsons, M. (2004) *Effective Knowledge Management for Law Firms*, Oxford University Press.

Rumizen, M. (2002) *The Complete Idiot's Guide to Knowledge Management*, CWL Publishing Enterprises.

Rusanow, G. (2003) *Knowledge Management and the Smarter Lawyer*, Incisive Media.

Schein, E. (1997) *Organisation Culture and Leadership*, Jossey-Bass.

Susskind, R. (2008) *The End of Lawyers? Rethinking the Nature of Legal Services*, Oxford University Press.

Sveiby, K. (1990) *Den Osynliga Balansrakningen* ('The Invisible Balance Sheet'), Affarsvarlden Forlag. Now out of print. Further details at **www.sveiby.com/library.html**.

Communities of practice

Wenger, Snyder and McDermott (2002) *Cultivating Communities of Practice*, Harvard University Press.

Measurement

Kusko, B. (1993) *Fuzzy Thinking: The New Science of Fuzzy Logic*, Hyperion.

Operations

Slack, N., Chambers, S. and Johnson, R. (2010) *Operations Management*, 6th edn, Financial Times, Prentice Hall.

PKM

Cope, M. (2000) *Know Your Value: Manage Your Knowledge and Make it Pay*, Prentice Hall.

RATER surveys

Hooley, G., Piercy, N. and Nicoulaud, B. (2008) *Marketing Strategy and Competitive Positioning*, 4th edn, Financial Times, Prentice Hall.

Social Network Analysis

Chaffey, D. and Wood, S. (2008) *Business Information Management*, Pearson Education Ltd.

Strategies

Porter, M.E. (1980) *Competitive Strategy: Techniques for Analyzing Industries and Competitors*, Free Press.
Porter, M.E. (1985) *Competitive Advantage: Creating and Sustaining Superior Performance*, Free Press.

Training

Daicoff, S. (2004) *Lawyer, Know Thyself: A Psychological Analysis of Personality Strengths and Weaknesses*, American Psychological Association Books.
Honey, P. and Mumford, A. (1982) *The Manual of Learning Styles*, Peter Honey Publications.
Honey, P. and Mumford, A. (1983) *Using Your Learning Styles*, Peter Honey Publications.
Kirkpatrick, D. (2006) *Evaluating Training Programs: The Four Levels*, 3rd edn, Berrett-Koehler Publishers.
Kolb, D. (1984) *Experiential learning: Experience as the source of learning and development*, Prentice-Hall.

Articles

Barth, S. (2003) 'Personal toolkit: A framework for PKM tools', *KM World*, 1 January, **www.kmworld.com/Articles/Editorial/Feature/Personal-toolkit-A-framework-for-personal-knowledge-management-tools-9416.aspx**.

Benetton, L. (2011) 'Knowledge management know-how', *Lawyers Weekly*, 5 August.

Blackler, F. (1995) 'Knowledge, knowledge work and organizations: an overview and interpretation', *Organisation Studies*, 16:6, 1021–46.

Frand, J. and Hixon, C. (1999) 'Personal knowledge management: Who, what, why, when, where, how?'. December 1999 (**www.anderson.ucla.edu/faculty/jason.frand/researcher/speeches/PKM.htm**).

Goodman, J. (2007) 'Training delivery: which route to choose?', *KIM Legal*, 16 October, 2.2.

Kaplan, R. and Norton, D. (1992) 'The balanced scorecard – measures that drive performance', *Harvard Business Review*, January-February 71–79.

Kaplan, R. and Norton, D. (2001) 'Transforming the Balanced Scorecard from Performance Measurement to Strategic Management: Part 1', *Accounting Horizons*, 15(1) March, 87–104.

Kumar, M. and Antony, J. (2007) 'Common myths of Six Sigma demystified', *International Journal of Quality and reliability management*, 25:8, 878.

Lillirank, P. (2002) 'The quality of information', *International Journal of Quality and Reliability Management*, 2:6, 691–703.

McDermott, R., Snyder, W. and Wenger, E. (2000) 'Community development as a natural step', *Knowledge Management Review*, Nov/Dec.

Nonaka, I. (1991), 'The knowledge creating company', *Harvard Business Review* November–December, 96–104.

OMC partners (2011) 'The knowledge imperative' March 2011 (**www.omc-partners.com/articles/The%20knowledge%20imperative.pdf**).

Pancucci, D. (2002) 'Harnessing the wind: Measuring KM', *Knowledge Management Magazine*, March, p. 12.

Rodwell, I. (2007) 'KM Support for clients: Building a better road', *KIM Legal*, May/June p. 24,

Russell, H (2007) 'The Power of Personality', *KIM Legal*, 16 October, 2:2.

Schroeder, R. et al (2008) 'Six Sigma: Definitions and underlying theory', *Journal of Operations Management*, 26, 536–554.

Snowden, D. (2002) 'Complex acts of knowing: Paradox and descriptive self-awareness', *Journal of Knowledge Management*, 6:2, 100–111.

Snowden, D. (2010) 'Enabling an ecological model, preferably with intelligence', *KIM Legal*, Dec 2010/Jan 2011, pp. 16–19.

Webber, A. (1993) 'What's so new about the new economy', *Harvard Business Review*, Jan-Feb: 27.

Twitter

Interesting people to follow

@charonqc
@davidgurteen
@gavward
@gebhardt
@glambert
@gnawledge
@heleneadby
@ju_summerhayes

@knowledgetank
@lawyercatrin
@lawyerist
@legalbizzle
@markgould13
@mashable
@millymoo
@matthoman
@weknowmore

Websites and blogs

www.gurteen.com
www.jarche.com
www.kmlegalmag.com
www.lawyerist.com
blog.tarn.org
www.theknowledgebusiness.co.uk
www.knowledgenetworkwest.com
knowledge4lawyers.wordpress.com
aboveandbeyondkm.com
lawyerkm.com
www.nickmilton.com
www.geeklawblog.com
kevin.lexblog.com

Useful work-related apps

Aroundme
Bump
Dragon dictation
Evernote
Hootsuite
imindmap
WordPress
Wikipanion

Index

169